D1158380

FANFARE FOR PUPPETS!

Muffin the Mule with Annette Mills and Ann Hogarth (*BBC copyright*)

FANFARE FOR PUPPETS!

A personal and idiosyncratic view
of the puppet theatre by

ANN HOGARTH

with technical sections by

JAN BUSSELL

David & Charles
Newton Abbot   London   North Pomfret (Vt)

Colour photography by Tony Griffiths
Photography 2000

British Library Cataloguing in Publication Data
Hogarth, Ann
  Fanfare for puppets!: a personal and
  idiosyncratic view of the puppet theatre.
  1. Puppets and puppet-plays
  I. Title II. Bussell, Jan
  791.5'3   PN1972

ISBN 0–7153–8723–5

Phototypeset by ABM Typographics Ltd, Hull
and printed in Great Britain
by Butler & Tanner Ltd, Frome
for David & Charles (Publishers) Limited
Brunel House   Newton Abbot   Devon

Published in the United States of America
by David & Charles Inc
North Pomfret   Vermont 05053   USA

CONTENTS

FOREWORD

As one man might write of his travels down the Ganges and not expect his readers to be all good oarsmen, or another of his adventures on the Himalayas for those who have never set foot on a mountain, so we have written of our journeyings for those who have never seen a puppet since childhood. We hope this book will catch the attention of people of very different interests and outlooks, telling as it does of individual and personal talents.

This is not a book intended for puppeteers or experts on the Puppet Theatre, although we hope many of them will enjoy it. It will not tell them much, if anything, they do not already know about the technical side of puppetry. For it is a book of personal experiences, an account of our journey through the world of the puppet players and their performances, of the people we have met and the shows we have seen. It is necessarily incomplete for it would be impossible to write of all the interesting personalities in the puppet world. We hope it may lead others to follow in our footsteps and also open up new paths for some.

The world is so small a place nowadays, and we tend to take our way of life with us wherever we go, so perhaps it will be of value to know something of the pockets of culture, creativity and thought that have survived, for centuries in some cases, in many parts of the world, and can still be found and enjoyed both by the knowledgeable traveller and the armchair reader.

INTRODUCTION

In the puppet we have all those elements necessary to interpretation and in the puppet stage every element necessary to a creative and fine art.

Gordon Craig, *The Art of the Theatre*

Let us be honest and acknowledge from the start that much of Puppet Theatre today (and maybe in the past also, who can tell?) is less than perfect. Nevertheless, scattered around the world can be found great traditions carried on by those rare individuals, the creative and gifted Puppet Masters, in whose hands puppets acquire a living magic that has fascinated audiences throughout history. What is it that has drawn these men to devote their lives to this sadly misunderstood and misused art form, and to discover in it such a powerful means of expression?

For them, and through them for their audiences, adults or children, a puppet is something more than a cleverly animated little figure – a clown, a harlequin or perhaps an animal. It is the embodiment of character, or of an idea, and the expression of the manipulator's personality. It is something more than the bringing to life of an inanimate object; it is in controlled movement that its full power is to be found – dramatic movement, the movement of the theatre. A figure which cleverly apes the everyday movements of human beings can be very entertaining for a short time as a technical tour de force, and there are many successful puppets in this category. But the true puppet does much more than this; its movements offer an artist's interpretative vision and comment on life. They are as carefully planned by the manipulator as the movements of an actor, or the steps of a ballet, and powerfully evoke the expression of an idea or a character. They are in fact creative.

Thus, though sculptor and manipulator must work in unison – indeed they are sometimes one and the same person – it is the manipulator who breathes the fire of life into the puppet. To him the puppet is a tool, like the musician's instrument, which he uses to express ideas. Each figure

7

he handles will embody a facet of his own personality. An equally great Puppet Master with the same script and the same figure cannot help but offer a different interpretation of the role, just as will different actors in the same part. So in going to the puppet theatre the most pleasurable and exciting experience is to be derived not from a comic simulation of reality, not from clever technical tricks, nor even from an excellence of carving: it is to be found in the acting and the 'message' of the manipulators. And it is precisely this aspect of puppetry which attracts the true artist.

Puppet Masters of high quality are as scarce as great actors, great painters or great musicians. But they do exist and have indeed exercised their personal, though evanescent, spells on mankind since very early times. To many people today puppetry conjures up pictures of children's hour television, and this modern sideline of employing puppets as something with which to keep the children quiet has achieved such momentum that many people accept the idea that this is all the art has to offer, and will scoff at the use of the word 'art' for such antics – and in this last they are, alas, often quite right. Of course creative puppetry is often produced and presented for children; but it is only too easy for a clever technician, with nothing to say, to attempt to hold their attention with what he calls 'audience participation' ('ee's be'ind yer! No! 'e ain't!) and for the success of his show to be judged by the amount of noise the children make.

In the early days of puppetry, hundreds of years ago, no Puppet Master would have dreamed of performing for children only. The shows were given for the community and everybody went. Before the majority of people could read or write puppetry was a means of expressing the religious, historical and moral traditions of a country. Legends were handed down from showman to showman, from generation to generation, and the puppet shows thus became the living history books, the showmen the scholars, the prophets, of their land. Puppetry was a natural development of story-telling and preaching, for it is related that the priests in China began to animate religious idols in order to bring more force to their doctrines and to attract more followers. Indeed a great deal of puppetry in the ancient world has a deeply religious and deeply sincere significance, the performances giving expression to a whole moral philosophy. The performances to this day in Java last all night long, presenting legendary tales of the battles of Gods and Princes, with philosophical comments; and before giving such a marathon the Dalang – the showman – must prepare himself with prayer and fasting. Only the other day we heard from a friend that she had asked some villagers in Java why they had travelled quite long distances to bring their children to such a show. 'How else will they learn these things? How else will they know how to behave?' was the reply.

No one can say with safety where puppets first started, but it is generally agreed that it was in the East, very likely in India. The ancient civilisations all had their puppet theatres, though of greatly differing kinds, which we shall show later; and traces of Indian culture, stories and characters from the great Hindu epics, the Mahabharata and the Ramayana, are found concealed and disguised in many of them. And of course it is always difficult to say where religious ceremony ends and theatrical performance begins. From the East the art spread to Turkey and Greece, and later to Italy and the whole of Europe. Gradually in this migration the religious aspect became lost. The showmen of Turkey and Greece replaced the traditional legends with up-to-date stories caricaturing local political leaders and generals of their day. Their theatres became the forerunners in a very elaborate manner of the modern political strip cartoon. They replaced the historical approach to puppetry with something more resembling the newspaper.

All this time, through the centuries, audiences too were changing. As people became better educated, the theatre began to be regarded as an artistic medium. Distinguished writers and poets became interested in puppets, wrote for them and even sometimes performed and experimented with them. In Japan the most famous of all its playwrights, Chikamatsu, who has been compared with Shakespeare in stature, wrote almost exclusively for puppets; and in Europe Goethe based his famous *Faust* on a puppet play, while George Sand gave puppet shows for intellectuals and Haydn wrote operettas for puppets.

But away from the intellectual movement, the Puppet Theatre was turning into a 'Puppet Show' and beginning to go downhill. Instead of making its home in the fashionable theatres and literary salons it was to be found in the music halls and fairgrounds; in England particularly it became a street-corner affair. The Codlin family of puppet players, whom Dickens describes in *The Old Curiosity Shop*, were very much vagabonds, if not rogues, and the plays, too, instead of being witty and intelligent, descended often into obscenity and coarse humour. By the beginning of this century the few travelling theatres of repute still existing were so hit by the pace of mechanical progress and by the cinema in particular, that it seemed the art would die out altogether.

Fortunately, however, perhaps as a counter to the very mechanics of the age, a new movement began to develop. In the 1920s in Paris, for instance, Princess de Polignac commissioned musicians such as Manuel de Falla and Stravinsky to write puppet operas for her salon theatre; Gordon Craig was drawing attention to the Puppet Theatre in his writings; and Bernard Shaw wrote a playlet expressly for marionettes. Artists, rather than vagrant showmen, began to play with puppets, especially in Eastern Europe, where such countries as Russia, Romania, Poland and Czechoslovakia can now boast elaborate state-owned puppet theatres with large staffs including musicians, carvers, designers and writers – the one in Moscow is reputed to have over 300 people on the payroll! Puppetry has come to be regarded in these countries as a cultural necessity, and besides having permanent specially designed theatres, companies are sent on tour, playing to children in the daytime and adults in the evening. Nowadays, too, even in the West, where puppets have become popular largely on television and in schools, they can sometimes be found playing adult material in their true home – the theatre.

In the following chapters we shall describe some of the different types of puppets to be found, their mechanics and the interesting people we have met performing with them.

1
GLOVE PUPPETS

My hand is the soul of the Puppet

. . . so says the great Russian Puppet Master, Sergei Obrastzov. He maintains that the glove puppet is superior to all other types because of the immediacy of the contact between showman and puppet, with no rods or strings to be manipulated. Be that as it may, the glove puppet, because it cannot be seen to be technically 'clever' must be very strongly characterised, its handling of properties meticulously rehearsed and reliable, its script entertaining and fast moving with a lot of practical business, and the showman, if he is working alone, must have a strong voice with which to portray several different characters, moving quickly from one to the other.

The glove puppet is basically a head, two hands and a costume. The head usually fits on the operator's first finger, with the hands on the thumb and middle finger. But this can be varied. The large and heavy Catalan puppets, for instance, are worked with the head fitted on the three middle fingers while the thumb and little finger take the hands. Sometimes, again, two fingers – the forefinger and the middle – are inserted in the head, giving a better turning movement. Of course the head must be specially made with the holes required of the right size to fit the operator's hands.

Glove puppets are usually seen in a booth which hides the showman. He will hang his puppets upside down on hooks placed so that he can slip his hands in or out of each as he needs them, and the properties and scenery for the play will stand on a shelf or be hung up so that he can easily reach them.

Probably the best known glove puppet in the world is Mr Punch who is a direct descendant through Pulcinella of the Comedia del Arte. He, with his wife Judy, his baby, the crocodile etc, has been performing for upwards of 300 years. Characters similar to Punch – with hooked noses,

Scene from The Hogarth Puppets production of *Two Slatterns and a King* by E. St Vincent Millais

humpbacks and squeaky voices, all deriving from the medieval strolling players, can be found in Russia (Petrushka), France (Polichinelle), Italy (Pulcinella) among others; and to them must be added national figures as Kasper of Germany, Kasparek of Czechoslovakia, Guignol of France, Hans Klassen of Holland and many others. These are all traditional or historical personalities and their characters and the type of plays they perform have remained more or less the same over many generations.

Very different traditional glove puppets are found in China, where they are known as 'bag' or 'sack' puppets. These exquisite, small puppets have a history going back hundreds of years, and some of the actual figures have been handed down for generations. We saw a performance by The Puppet Theatre of Peking when they were visiting Paris some years ago and, on making ourselves known to the performers, were invited to watch a show backstage. The puppets are very small, with delicate porcelain hands and faces, dressed in beautiful silks and brocades. They are manipulated with breathtaking skill – duelling, juggling, fighting with dragons – performing the same traditional legends as can be seen in the human theatres. The puppets are only about 20 to 25cm (8 to 10in) high and so can only be played before small audiences.

Backstage we found the performers most friendly. They sat on small stools, smiling and drinking from mugs. We couldn't speak to them at all, but we sat with them and were each given a steaming drink. Jan drank a little and mimed ecstasy – never had he tasted anything so delicious! 'Don't overdo it,' I cautioned him. 'Why? What is it?' 'Hot water,' I told him. We watched the Chinese as they sat playing with their puppets, practising the movements of the small figures, sometimes tossing one into the air and catching it unerringly on the correct fingers. We feared for those delicate porcelain heads but they never let one fall. Later they opened chests and showed us the beautiful costumes ready to be put on the puppets as the play progressed.

This company we saw in Paris was only a small one but there are much larger troupes to be found, in which one can occasionally see battles between massed armies, calling perhaps for twenty manipulators. In the press of battle a figure may get pushed above the mob and flung into the air, to be nimbly caught by another manipulator on the far side of the stage. Such skills are of course the result of long training – years spent in special schools where the manipulation of puppets is taught, and where the knowledge and experience of many generations is handed down.

Before we leave the traditional glove puppets and move on to look at our present times, there are two interesting characters we must mention, one in France and the other in Italy. The French one is Guignol,

A Chinese glove puppet production in Peking

created in Lyons about 1810 by Laurent Mourguet. Guignol was a lace-maker's apprentice, a typical working-class young man of the area and he immediately captured the affections of the Lyonnaises. Unlike our Mr Punch who has always appeared in only one play, the Guignol show-men present him in a variety of plots. He is always a cheerful, helpful young man, usually going about his master's business when adventure or misfortune strikes him. There are literally hundreds of Guignol scripts, with titles such as: *Guignol on the Moon: Guignol and the Devil's Bridge: Guignol and the Golden Hand: Guignol and the Serpent: Guignol and the Dungeons of the Old Castle.* Needless to say in every play he is always triumphant and survives to fight another day. He has a close friend, Gnaffron, and a wife, Madelon. Guignol is so well known throughout France that the word 'guignol' has become synonymous with the word for puppet and is, in fact, the word mostly used. Practically every city park has its Guignol Theatre and there is a Guignol Museum in Lyons. A certain type of melodrama popular in the real theatre during the nineteenth and early twentieth centuries became known, even in Britain, as Grand Guignol, as opposed to the puppet Guignol.

The Italian character, Gioppino, is interesting for a very different reason. He is the local puppet hero of Bergamo, a medieval town of great charm and interest set in lovely mountainous country in northern Italy. Here, in the Old Town, there developed a strong Puppet Theatre in the nineteenth century, with several companies playing to the local population. Many of the large, highly coloured and beautifully dressed puppets survive today, though they do not perform very often, and one sometimes sees them for sale in antique shops. If you look at them you will see many of the characters have highly exaggerated goitres on their necks – known locally as 'potatoes'. There are, for instance, figures of Gioppino himself as a baby, as a soldier, as a handsome young man etc, but on all of them he has these monstrous growths, as do all the puppets representing his family and friends. There are other puppets, however, in the same plays which do not have these deformities. They are the local aristocracy, the educated and the well-to-do. Apparently at the time when these puppets were being made and the plays performed, a serious deficiency of iodine, minerals etc in the food and water supply caused this affliction. The working men's families, eating a poor diet and drinking snow water (deficient in iodine) all suffered from it, whilst the well-to-do with a much better and more varied diet could not only resist the disease, but if they succumbed could afford medical attention and remedies. So these puppets are making a vivid social comment on

14

Gioppino from Bergamo, Italy

the times in which they were made and performed. Perhaps they may even have helped to draw attention to the plight of their operators and hastened the discovery of a cure!

In many places in this century, and in particular since World War II, a new generation of performers has arisen presenting very varied repertoires, many of them with glove puppets. In Russia the most famous living Puppet Master, Sergei Obrastzov, has for years been presenting his delightful solo show all over the world, his puppets varying from ballad-singing monkeys and dogs, an hilarious though brief take-off of 'Carmen', a Tamer who tempts once too often his man-eating Tiger, to a very realistic Baby sung to sleep with a Russian lullabye, and a superb vodka-drinking Drunk. One outstanding item is a love scene between Obrastzov's two bare hands, each with a simple ball on the forefinger to represent the head. His performances are always accompanied by his wife, Olga, at the piano.

Another Puppet Master to play with his bare hands is the French-

The Drunkard by Sergei Obrastzov

man, Yves Joly, who sometimes uses the hands of several operators to perform ballets or mimes to music, and gives one charming item in which two gloved hands – one male, one female – help each other to undress before going swimming. Joly also uses umbrellas as characters, enacting an entire love story with the City Gent Umbrella, the Frivolous Parasol, the Dashing Hero, the Dowdy Ma-in-law etc.

A performer in quite a different style was Therese Keller of Switzerland. She was a very talented and very dedicated performer, playing charming tales and legends, mostly to children. We saw one of these performances in a small town where an extremely rowdy and unruly audience of about 500 were all gathered in a hall, shouting and shoving. 'Poor Therese', we thought. 'What a time she's going to have!' But far from it. As soon as she started to perform they were held spellbound. She played quietly, but with great sympathy and conviction. Her booth had two playing areas, one above the other, which created good dramatic pictures, with the puppets able to lean down or gaze up at each other. She also had a great feeling for the relationship of one figure to another; a tall figure striding beside a smaller, trotting one; or a king offering

Yves Joly with company and puppets

comfort to a lowly servant, all very strongly characterised and defined. She added dignity to the appearance of her characters by lengthening their arms with tubes within their costumes.

Therese Keller told us that she decided to be a puppet player when she was about eight years old, and from then on she practised each day, stretching every joint in her hands and extending the reach between her fingers, so that her puppets would have a good shape and do the many things that she required of them with style and credibility. She certainly succeeded. This attention to detail and rounding of the personalities of the puppets is one thing that distinguishes the great from the ordinary performer.

Kasper and Old Lady by Therese Keller (*photo: Erismann, Bern*)

Glove puppets get very hard wear during performances and need to be strongly made if they are to be used professionally, giving perhaps six, eight or even more shows a week and, if it is a touring company, being constantly packed and unpacked. They are in fact 'tools of trade' and should be as well made and reliable as a craftsman's treasured tool. But occasionally one comes across someone who makes and performs with puppets purely for their own pleasure and satisfaction. We once met two ladies who lived in a barn in Surrey and made the heads of their delicate little glove puppets from eggshells! For the performance one of them stood outside the booth and sang unaccompanied narrative ballads, which the other illustrated with the puppets. On the day we visited them they were in great distress as a favourite duck had failed to lay the greenish egg needed for the head of the sickly Lord Randall:

. . . Mother make my bed soon
For I'm wearied with hunting and fain would lie down.

Except for the Chinese battle scenes mentioned above and Yves Joly's hands, nearly all the shows we have described have been operated by one Puppet Master, but of course this need not be so. Plays calling for

18

more than two characters on stage at once will necessitate enlarging the company. But this in turn means enlarging the booth and even perhaps the vehicle which transports it and the company. So it is a question of logistics. Very spectacular effects can be achieved with large numbers of glove puppets moving in unison. About twenty years ago a Polish company, Arlekin from Lodz, directed by Henryk Ryl, visited England for the first time. They brought a programme of folk songs and dances. They were a company of about twelve men and girls, who sang the traditional work and play songs of Poland and between them could muster twenty-four puppets on stage all moving together through the dances in their bright national costumes. The effect was stunning and English audiences, who had never seen anything like it, were absolutely delighted.

In Russia and Romania, too, we have seen shows employing large numbers of figures. The booths and stages have also been developed. We have watched puppets perform round the edge of a huge tilted circle, the manipulators being in the centre. Sometimes the stage consists of three or more different levels of scenery, each one higher than the one in front. The operators work hidden behind the rows of scenery, raised on rostrums so that they can reach above it. The drawback to this style of presentation is that the audience cannot sit in balconies or circles as the operators are then revealed. This of course applies to all types of puppet worked from below.

In the very large state-supported theatres of Eastern Europe most spectacular shows are staged, with scenery coming and going, massed choirs of puppets, orchestras, armies and chorus lines all deployed as in a Hollywood musical. These shows amaze at first, but there is a certain similarity when one has seen several. Then one is glad to find again a one- or two-man set-up where there is time for characterisation to be developed and for the audience to be intrigued and delighted as the puppets make their comment on the human race and mock its foolish ways.

In Germany the counterpart to Mr Punch is called Kasper, but he is a more charming and likeable character, and his performances have a gentler and less bawdy brand of humour. One of the most famous exponents of Kasper was the much loved and admired Puppet Master, Max Jacob, who founded the Hohensteiner troupe. Jacob had a tremendous influence on the whole German puppet movement, training several generations of students, who can now be found all over the world (we have met them in Canada, Hawaii and New Zealand) perpetuating his ideas and methods. Kasper shows also differ from Punch's in that they

Italo Ferrari (1877–1961) of Parma, Italy, with traditional puppets

play many different stories, each showman having his own repertoire.

Going south to Italy we find that the Ferrari troupe of Parma, whilst still playing in the style of the Comedia del Arte, has more or less dropped the character of Pulcinella. This company plays in a large booth with five or six manipulators, in a very lively, excitable style. The puppets are large with big heads. They often have moving eyes and mouths and are painted in a very exaggerated, masklike style. The production moves at a great pace, entirely a family affair, and at one show we watched backstage at the Regie Theatre, Parma, three or four generations were taking part. There was loud music and vivid scenery and lighting effects. The scenery was painted on paper, in what used to be the traditional Continental way, and in the rapid changes often got torn. While the show was still going on two smallish grandchildren laid it out on the stage floor of the theatre and rapidly and efficiently mended it with Sellotape ready for its next appearance.

But Pulcinella himself can still be seen in Italy. During the performance of an open-air show in a square by the side of a fruit market in a small Italian town there occurs the inevitable traditional chase. But it is a chase with a difference, for when Pulcinella escapes behind some scenery he bursts out again – human size – from the side of the booth. Bruno Leone, masked and dressed as Pulcinella, dashes through the screaming audience tumbling over chairs and children, rampages round the market stalls stealing bananas and peaches and finally allows himself to be caught and pushed back into the booth to finish the show. Pulcinella is in fact very much alive.

In quite a different style and with a very modern approach to Puppet Theatre was the work of the Frenchman, Jean-Loup Temporal. He came under the influence of both Jacob and Obrastzov, but developed his own individual art. His children's shows were delightful and he was popular in many countries. He set himself very high standards and we were amazed to what lengths these would take him. Some years ago he mounted a production of a play *Le Tueur Sans Gage* by Ionesco of which we saw an early performance. When sometime later we enquired how it was going he replied, 'Oh, I burnt it! It wasn't good enough.' He had destroyed it all – puppets, scenery, everything. Alas, he died last year, so now it will never be made.

Puppet by Jean-Loup Temporal for *Le Tueur Sans Gage* by Eugene Ionesco (*photo: Dominique Temporal*)

Le Manteau from France

But of course, like other arts, the Puppet Theatre never stands still, and new forms and ideas are always being introduced and developed, even into so simple a form as the glove puppet play. For instance, another Frenchman, Jean Paul Hubert, turns himself into a walking theatre. He heightens himself several inches by wearing huge sabots carved and painted as swans or ducks; his booth hangs from his shoulders, so that his face is hidden, and his body is literally hung about with all the puppets, gadgets, musical instruments, strange creatures etc, that he will use in the show. It is all very cleverly worked out and he gives an extremely fast-moving and funny performance.

Another clever idea comes from Bjorn Fühler. The show is billed as 'Le Manteau' and that is exactly what his theatre is – a Coat. He is within it and the various characters emerge from the pockets and other apertures to present an amusing and witty story of a journey. In another programme this innovative performer, in the guise of a philosophic 'down and out' presents a circus, amongst other extraordinary feats manipulating performing animals on his feet whilst the puppets on his hands put them through their paces.

Sitting in the auditorium waiting for the start of the performance by

Figurentheater Triangel from Holland

the Triangel Theatre of Holland, one can have no conception of the
terrors that lie ahead. When the pink lights are faded out and the cosy-
appearing proscenium has vanished, we are confronted with an almost
claustrophobically small booth. They play with several different types of
puppet. Nothing that appears is what it seems, almost all is macabre if
not evil. Playing without words, almost without sound, never to children, Henk and Ans Boerwinkel build up a remarkable atmosphere of

23

A 'Picasso' puppet by The Hogarth Puppets

horror and tension. Every character is fully developed and utterly believable. From some one recoils, with others one suffers. With a programme of some twenty brief items they have won an enormous international reputation.

For many years now latex rubber has been available and has made possible the construction of very large puppet heads, light and easy to handle and able to screw up their faces into all sorts of possible and impossible grimaces. Obrastzov, for instance, was quick to seize upon it to make a new head for his famous Drunkard who was thereafter able to leer and contort his face in an even more horrible and amusing manner. We have made several of these large heads, including two Gargoyles who – in a poem by Clive Sansom – complain of the drought and welcome an approaching storm which enables them to 'spit on the Churchmen hurrying under'. The temptation to use 'real water' was too great for us and the resulting paraphernalia of gutters, plastic bottles, pipes and hot water bottles made it so complicated that we hardly ever performed it. For the Churchmen 'hurrying under' we used shadow puppets, described in Chapter 2.

We made three others of these large rubber heads to use as Prologues to the show. One, Rufus the Clown, introduced children's shows, particularly in our caravan theatre, where he used to appear up on the roof. He proved very popular, with his red hair and ability to pull funny faces and egg on the children to do the same back. We had a young student from Poland to help us with these caravan shows one year, who enquired, 'Is he called Roofus because he comes out of the roof?'

Another character was a medieval Seller of Cures, again to a poem by Clive Sansom. It took both of us to manipulate him, one taking the head and the other the hands. We used to show him without any masking and wore black hoods to hide our faces, which we found very hot and uncomfortable, so, like the Gargoyles, we didn't perform with him often.

Yet a third such rubber head we made 'after a painting by Picasso' using him as a Prologue to adult shows with a verse expressing our wish that the public wouldn't always think of puppets as 'only for children':

I am a Puppet of a Portrait of a Poet
Painted by Picasso. Presented with a Purpose.
The Problem of Puppets at the Present Period
Is the Prejudice of the Populace we are Puerile.
This is Patently Piffle
For the Proper Performance of the Puppet
Is to Portray the Peculiarities of People –
Prince, Proletarian, Priest or Politician.
And for these Portrayals to be Properly Appreciated
Presumes a Pre-knowledge by our Public of the Persons so Presented.
This the Precious Poppets of Proud Parents cannot Possibly Possess.
We Puppets therefore Prayerfully Plead
That as Picasso's Portraits for the Parlour
Not the Playpen you may Purchase –
So the Parent – not the Piccaninny –
Is the Puppet's Proper Public.

A.H.

We have come a long way from the familiar Punch and Judy booth, standing in the town square or on the beach, offering the old, old story to its ever faithful public. Now we will take a look at what goes on in a very different world – that of the shadow puppet.

2
SHADOW PUPPETS

A brilliant light and a clean sheet is a great attraction and it's the attraction is everything.

Galantee Showman
Mayhew's Characters

In the shadow puppet theatre the spectator sees only the shadow of the puppet not the figure itself. The basic requirements for a performance are simple: a screen of semi-transparent material – cotton, linen, silk, plastic or even tracing paper are all suitable – and a light placed so that when a figure is held against the screen it gives a clear picture on the other side, but the source of the light is not seen by the audience. The figures themselves can be made of thick paper, cardboard, leather, plastic or thin metal, cut in bold silhouette, freely jointed and operated by rods either horizontally or from below. The figures can be decorated with lace-like patterns or be solid black and white, depending on their outline for characterisation. The shadow screen must be raised up so that the audience has a clear view of it, and should be masked with curtains or something similar to hide the operators.

The shadow puppet theatre is a particularly good medium for fantasy, for story-telling, for tales where the characters embark on long journeys etc. It can also be used effectively for social comment or for political cartoons, and with modern lighting techniques – such as quartz-iodine lamps or back projection – some very exciting developments are taking place. The use of several different sources of light and coloured filters can be dramatic and exciting, and even produce three-dimensional effects.

The beginnings of shadow puppets are very ancient and very obscure, but almost certainly started in China, though the Puppet Theatre in some other form may have arrived there from Greece with the early traders. The Chinese word for puppet – *k'wi-lei* – we are told is traceable

Setschuan shadow puppet from the collection of Max Bührmann

to medieval Greek. The Chinese themselves claim up to 2,000 years of performances with shadows, although only 1,000 years can be substantiated, with accounts of shows in the Sung and Ming dynasties. There is a charming legend from an even earlier millennium which tells that when during the Han dynasty the emperor's favourite concubine died, he was inconsolable until a young priest created a shadow figure of the dead woman. The movements and posturings of this puppet so delighted the bereaved monarch that he bestowed upon the priest-magician the title of 'Master of Learned Perfection'.

The Chinese Shadow Theatre has always been based on the classical stage of the human actors, and performs the same plays. The character of each puppet is easily identifiable – nobility, villainy, servility etc being obvious to the audience by its appearance before it even speaks,

27

and rank or occupation is shown by the colours or decorations it wears. There are still today shadow shows to be seen in China, the two principal being those of Peking with delicate highly coloured figures about 30cm (12in) high, and the much larger ones from Setschuan which are about 60cm (2ft) high. They both perform the same classical repertoire and have much the same design and movements – at least to the untutored Western eye. The puppets from Setschuan are more highly articulated than those from Peking. Dr Max Bührmann who had a very fine collection of those from Setschuan used to give performances all over Europe with them keeping as closely as possible to the original presentations, using Chinese rough silk for the screen and Chinese musical accompaniments.

Once when attending a seminar in Switzerland we met up with Dr Bührmann and, with his little English and our less German, he tried to explain to us various niceties of the Setschuan technique. At last, full of frustration, he snatched a sheet off his bed and rigging it up on the balcony in a moment, gave us a graphic demonstration by the light of the full moon.

We have seen a performance by the Peking Shadow Puppets in Paris where we watched storks, bears, monkeys, tortoises etc, as well as human characters, all manipulated with a marvellous skill and a great deal of humour. We have also seen a performance of Peking-style shadows which had been carried by emigrants to Taiwan and there been taken over by a young French girl, Anne Riston, who still performs the classical plays with the figures and scenery faithful to their origins of a thousand years earlier. In this Taiwanese/French show there was an incident when a Huntsman had to shoot down several 'suns' from the sky, and it was incredible to watch this tiny, highly coloured figure draw an arrow from the quiver on his back, place it in position in his bow, then with apparently immense strength let the arrow fly straight up to hit the errant 'sun'. This then tumbled to earth, split open and turned into a fantastic bird. The whole manoeuvre was then repeated until all the unwanted 'suns' had been destroyed – all achieved by a single manipulator. The patience, time and skill needed for this is amazing.

Whether shadow puppets travelled on to India from China or whether there were quite separate developments will never be known, but certainly the two styles of theatre are so very different that we are inclined to think there was no connection. Indian shadow puppets are mostly very large, up to 1·2 or 1·5m (4 or 5ft) high. As with all traditional shadow puppets they are made of hide – goat, calf, donkey or buffalo, intricately perforated and stained, according to tradition, with vegetable dyes. The women characters for instance are in hues of yellow, orange and brown, and Prince Rama is always a maroon colour as he is described in the Ramayana as being a dark person.

The screen in the old Indian Shadow Theatres was made of two saris pinned together with thorns and stretched between bamboo poles. Light used to be provided by a row of coconut shells containing oil and as the performances were given in the open air the flickering of these lamps must have given an added life to the scene. The plays are always based on the Ramayana or the Mahabharata. Nowadays things are not so romantic, the screen usually being of plastic and the lovely flickering flames replaced by fluorescent tubes.

But much of the traditional feeling still remains. In Milan recently we met up with Meher Contracter who has worked such wonders to keep alive the Indian Puppet Theatre. She and her troupe of shadow players from Ahmedabad were performing the day after us, and it transpired someone was ill and they were short of an operator. I was asked to step into the breach, and although not required to do much it was marvellous to be part of such an ancient tradition. Before the performance began everyone removed their shoes and Meher moved around the whole stage area several times, swinging a censer and praying for all the different elements present for the performance – the building, the audience, the operators, the stage, the puppets, the musicians with their instruments were all prayed for. The elephant-headed god – Shri Ganesh – renowned for his wisdom, was being invoked for his help. Then the performance began and continued in an atmosphere of marvellous harmony and happiness, everyone engrossed in their part, but at the same time keeping a watchful eye for the well-being of the others. It was a most enjoyable experience, and one was very conscious of the religious element in the performance.

'O Lord let me be a Wayang in your hands', so wrote a Javanese poet. 'Wayang' means performance, but it is also used as the word for puppet and the Shadow Puppet Theatre of Java is one of the oldest which can still be seen performing today. It is almost timeless, part of a religious and cultural heritage in which the stylised figures, so fantastic to Western eyes, and the heroic sagas they perform, have not altered for about a thousand years. New puppets, exact replicas of the old, are still being made today; in fact it is impossible often for even an expert to date a figure, so alike and so durable are they. Their legends are reverently handed on word for word from showman to showman. The

Shadow puppet from Andhra, India; Sita from the Ramayana is over 300 years old

Dalang, as he is called, is regarded almost as a priest, the living history book of ancient Java, a man of great learning and wisdom.

The Javanese puppet play is much more than mere entertainment. It expresses a whole philosophy, and was a means of educating an illiterate people in ethics, morals, art, politics and religion. A performance was – and to some extent still is – more akin to a religious observance than a theatrical display. Its impact is considered still so strong that recently official attempts have been made to bring its teaching and content more in line with the thinking of a twentieth-century republican state.

Opinion differs as to the origin of these shows. They may have started as a form of ancestor worship – until recently the puppets were regarded by the country folk as materialised silhouettes of ancestral ghosts; or they may have been connected with ancient tribal initiation rites sacred to the men, who were originally the only people permitted to watch the performances. They sat always behind the Dalang and so saw the actual puppets. When the women and children were eventually admitted they had to sit on the opposite side of the screen and see only the shadows of the puppets. This convention is not now strictly adhered to.

Many of the stories performed are of Indian origin, though long since rendered Javanese in spirit and character. We do not know if the puppets originally came from India also, but with their highly individual design this seems unlikely.

The 'shadow' shows are called Wayang Kulit – literally 'Skin or Hide Performance'. The figures are very large and beautifully designed, made out of leather and they vary in height from about 45 to 76cm (18 to 30in). These puppets are commonly known as shadow figures because of the exquisitely delicate filigree shadows they produce on the white cotton screen against which they perform. The effect is produced by a lace-like stencilling cut right through the leather, outlining and enhancing every detail of the costume. But, as we have said, it is not these strikingly beautiful shadows which the men have always watched. They sit on the showman's side of the screen, and the puppets are in fact painted in vivid colours – colours which are of course completely invisible in their black silhouettes. The shadows in fact went unwatched until the admission of the women and children only a few generations ago.

A Wayang Kulit figure has three rods. The main rod, which supports the body, is made of horn, and is split from the handle upwards, with the figure inserted between the two halves. The rod then curves through the design of the figure to a tapering point in the headdress, being fastened at intervals with fibre thongs. The handle, which is often ornate, ends in a sharp point about 30cm (12in) below the puppet's feet. The other rods are generally of wood, one to each hand, loosely attached with fibre.

The cutting of the stencil design is an extremely important part in the making of a puppet. There are no less than twelve chisel motifs, and if a wrong one were employed on, say, a part of a puppet's headdress or back sash, the audience would spot it immediately. The cutting of the nose and mouth and the angle of the head on the shoulders are all of character-giving significance, and must be exactly right for each individual. But the eye is considered the most important of all, and is always left till last. For with the eye as witness to everything the artist finally gives reincarnated life to the god or prince or warrior he is expressing. The painting of the puppets is equally important and must be carried out in a

31

prescribed sequence. Traditionally the puppet maker himself must live apart from his fellows while engaged on this work, pray much, only eat certain foods and dress in white. The colours of the puppet face, like the design of the figure as a whole, are highly stylised; red, white, gold, black and occasionally blue, are used, and indicate to the audience the temperament or state of mind of the character. One may find the same character in a different colour to suit a different part of an epic, as he reacts to events.

Of the many cycles of legends performed probably the oldest are those known as the Wayang Purwa. These are the stories based on the Hindu epics – the Ramayana and the Mahabharata. Performances are enormously long, lasting from sundown to sunrise. All the puppets are operated by the Dalang alone, and he also speaks for all of them and chants lengthy passages of narrative. A performance is not only a feat of memory for him but a feat of endurance. One might imagine that it was a feat of endurance for the audience as well, but this is not so. For though they will give certain scenes in which they are especially interested an astonishingly rapt and concentrated attention, they may walk away and miss a whole section. The performances are often held in some important household on the occasion of an event such as a birth or wedding, and besides the sacred rites to be attended to – of which the performance is considered one – there is also feasting going on. Jan, when attending one such occasion, was constantly being given little delicacies of obscure ingredients, wrapped in green leaves, passed to him underneath the screen by the solicitous women on the other side. Furthermore there are occasional lighthearted scenes interwoven with comical characters, who may even have some topical wisecracks to add, which keep the less serious minded in fits of laughter. Then there are the battles and duels which can be truly thrilling to watch, even to ourselves knowing nothing of the language, when the huge puppets are thrashed rhythmically against the screen, and deliver really violent blows upon each other. To be amongst the audience on the occasion of a performance is said to confer a blessing in itself.

During the performance the Dalang sits cross legged facing the screen, which is about 3·65m (12ft) wide and 1·2m (4ft) high, stretched on a framework some 60cm (2ft) above the ground. Behind him and to the sides are the Gamelan players – an orchestra of some twelve to twenty-four gongs and xylophonic instruments. The Dalang is, in addition to his other duties, the conductor, giving them the beat by clanking two pieces of metal together with his left heel on the puppet box,

32

Orlando, Angelica and Astolfo, traditional puppets from Palermo in Sicily

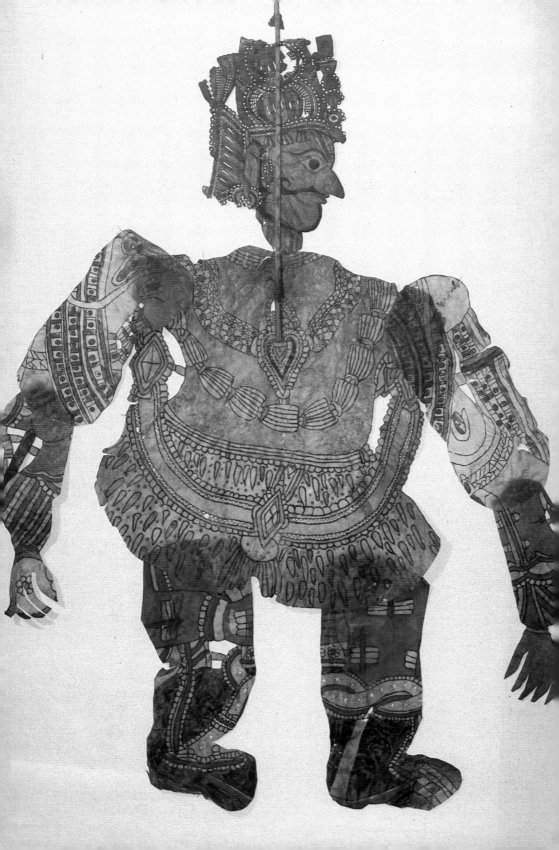

against which he sits. He often emphasises his speech and enhances the battles with this same rhythmic clanking. The puppets themselves are displayed in two forest-like groups against the screen to the sides, their horn handles dug into the soft pith of a large palm or banana trunk secured along the base of the screen. The smallest figures are placed nearest the centre, but there is no convention here, as in some traditional puppet theatres, that the smallest is the least important. Indeed, one of the holiest and wisest of the Wayang Purwa figures – Deva Ruchi – is also one of the smallest. But which side the figures are placed on is important and of great significance. On the right are all the noble and refined characters, with dark, white or gilt faces. On the left the coarser, mostly red-faced puppets, whose heads are not held so graciously on such elegant long necks, are assembled.

In the centre of the screen is placed the Gunungan. This is a large fan-shaped object, also made from leather, and finely patterned and with a horn handle. The design on it varies, but always depicts the Tree of Life, with sundry mythological devils, birds and beasts woven in and around the foliage and roots. The Gunungan has a three-fold purpose. It is used before and after the performance in much the same way as we use a drop-curtain. At the beginning of the show the Dalang can indicate to the audience, by holding it at a particular angle, the location of the scene to be played; and during the action it may be used to represent a piece of scenery, say a rock or a gateway. Sometimes it is waved from side to side behind the figures to indicate they are going on a journey, or shaken against a flickering light to indicate fire.

The Purwa stories are concerned with the trials and tribulations, battles and triumphs of five noble brothers, the Pandawa, and their friend and counsellor Prince Kresna, who is one of the reincarnations of Prince Rama. Together they represent all that is good and virtuous, and therefore take up their position on the Dalang's right. The adversaries they will meet in their search for truth stand opposite them, on the Dalang's left – giants, apes and men of bold character but lesser ideals. In every story right will triumph. The primitive people for whom they were originally performed learned through them to believe in the ultimate value of virtue in thought and deed.

Also ranged on the left, but by no means because they are bad, are Semar and his sons Gareng and Petruk, described variously as clowns,

Prince Rama, a large shadow puppet from Andhra, India

35

Nang shadow puppet from Thailand

court jesters, scholars and disciples. Semar is believed by some to have
been a powerful god in the pre-Hindu mythology of Java. He is the most
sacred of the puppets and members of the audience are always reaching
out as they pass to touch the little fur top-knot he carries on his
forehead, so that it often has a rather bald and shabby appearance.

Everything about these shows is symbolic; from the screen which represents the universe, to the bronze lamp called a *blentjong* which
provides the source of light and is in the shape of a mythical bird representing the steed of the god Vishnu. Altogether a set of puppets for the
Wayang Purwa should have not less than 144 figures, this being the
number of human passions and characteristics. Every performance
opens and closes with a traditional chanted prologue and epilogue, and
before he starts the Dalang should pray. At the end of the show the
puppets should traditionally be laid in trays lined with peacocks'
feathers to protect them from evil influences (and insects too). Even the
plays themselves are divided into three parts, symbolic of the stages in
the life of a man. The introduction represents youth and impetuosity;

36

the middle part in which the complications of the plot develop, are compared with man's growth and thinking; and the third part, the dénouement, goes with the insight and wisdom achieved with old age. Something of the mystery and excitement which the showman-priest conjures into these figures seems to remain with them, even when they are transported thousands of miles and held in alien hands. As you hold them you feel they are far more than dolls, nearer perhaps to idols or saintly relics.

There was an interesting development of the Wayang Kulit in Thailand (Siam), although nowadays it is probably only to be found in museums. This is the shadow play called Nang – literally 'Hide Figures'. These shadow puppets are very large, between 90cm (3ft) and 1.5m (5ft) high and are not jointed or articulated in any way. They are purely pictorial, cut out of the hide full-face to the audience, embellished with the most elaborate and delicate tracery and depicted in dramatic poses which give the appearance of movement in the flickering flames of the

Javanese shadow puppet (*Collection Max Bürhmann*)

bonfires by which they are lit. Sometimes one piece comprises several characters, including animals such as tigers and elephants. All are supported by two rigid rods which are split and the figure fixed in between. Each is worked by one man. At first the Nang were shown against enormous white screens, and the operators would sway and bend and finally dance, holding the great puppets like huge fans above their heads. Gradually the screen was dispensed with and the men danced in the night, they and the figures illuminated by huge log fires. Each operator adopted in his movements characteristics similar to that of the puppet he was holding and moved sideways to give a two-dimensional effect as if they were still against a screen.

The plays performed were always from the Ramayana and told of Rama and Sita and Hanuman the Monkey. They were preceded by ceremonial invocations and offerings of candles to the Hindu gods. After an overture 'Ushering in the early evening monkeys', the play itself commenced. As in India and Java from whence they came, an air of solemnity and mystery pervaded the whole performance.

There is nothing at all religious or mystical about the Shadow Puppet Theatre in Turkey, where it arrived from the East, probably via Egypt. It may have been established in Turkey as early as the fourteenth century, but it is not until the sixteenth that we have reports of shows. The theatre is dominated by a character named Karagöz. He is a down-to-earth, rumbustuous, likeable fellow, of gypsy origins, with a loud, distinctive voice, speaking the language of the streets. His name means 'Black Eye' and this is his dominant feature. He also wears a huge hat which when knocked off, as it frequently is, discloses a completely bald head – always good for a laugh. He has a quick wit, is always up to some shady business or other, often in trouble, but in the end emerges triumphant.

The plays of the Karagöz theatre are based on folk tales with the addition of topical jokes and references, much social comment, but no politics. Karagöz features in all of them with his constant companion Hacivad, a much more cultivated, educated and altogether more refined character, and the contrast between these two is the basis of much of the humour. Like the Chinese, the Turks have a rather whimsical tale to explain the origin of the Shadow Theatre and of course Karagöz is the hero of it. He was a stonemason and was employed on the building of a new mosque for the Sultan. But he and his friend Hacivad spent all their time yarning, telling tall stories and capping each other's jokes. They were such an amusing pair that their fellow workmen spent more time listening to them and laughing at them than they did working.

Turkish shadow puppets – Hacivad and Karagöz

Until at last the Sultan in a rage ordered them to be executed. But when his command had been carried out, and all was quiet and the labourers back at their work, he felt remorseful and became greatly depressed, for he too had enjoyed their stories and repartee. To cheer him up the Overseer of the building works made two figures out of camel skin, of Karagöz and Hacivad, and casting their shadows on a screen rigged up on a balcony, re-enacted their conversations and antics to the delight of the Sultan and his workmen.

The showman in Turkey – the Karagödschi – usually works alone and must have at least twenty-eight plays in his repertoire, as performances are traditionally given every evening for the month of Ramadan. He must also be an excellent mime with a strong voice, able to give each character the distinctive accent for his station in life and the district he comes from. There are a large number of stock characters, all types well known to the public. As each character makes his appearance he will probably enter singing, and the audience will know immediately who is coming. The figures are about 30cm (12in) high, made of camel skin treated until it is almost transparent and painted in rich colours. Previous shadow puppets we have written about have all been worked by two or three rods from below, but in the Karagöz theatre the rods are held horizontally, pressing the figure against the screen. Most of them only have one rod, fixed to the body, but Karagöz himself always has two, the second going to his hand. The showman can hold both these rods in one hand when he needs to work a second character with the other.

The shadow screen nowadays is usually only about 107cm (3ft 6in) wide x 76cm (2ft 6in) high and consists of a frame covered with fine Egyptian cotton, screened below and at each side by Turkish carpets. Originally and ideally the light should be an oil lamp burning olive oil.

In Bursa near the Sea of Marmora there is now a statue to Karagöz, as tradition has it that he was born and died there. The statue gives an impression of a shadow screen showing the figures of Karagöz and Hacivad. Many of the common folk in Turkey used to believe that they had been real people who became known by their wit and cunning. It is sad that nowadays the tradition of the theatre seems to be dying out, performances are only given at children's parties, and there are no showmen in Turkey able to make a living with Karagöz.

As a relic of Turkish occupation the Shadow Theatre took root in Greece, where it is still active. Known as Karaghiosis it is complete with the hero's companion, known as Hadjiavatis, who has become a Town Crier. But the plays are different, based on Greek stories, with characters from the different country regions, all well known to the audiences. There is a lot of political and social comment included as well as satire, and the effect is rather that of a newspaper cartoon. The humour is very broad slapstick as Karaghiosis and Hadjiavatis stagger from one crisis to another, and as usual the old rogue wins through in the end.

The Greeks use a very much larger screen than the Turks – between 3·7m (12ft) and 4·6m (15ft) wide and 2·1m (7ft) high, made of white cotton. With a screen this size there is room for scenery and Karaghiosis' house can stand on one side and that of his victim for any particular play, opposite. The puppets are also much larger, 60 or 90cm (2 or 3ft) high and made of skin, either camel or sometimes pig, treated to make it semi-transparent. A great improvement over the Turkish figures is that they can be made to turn round on the stage by means of a hinge at the shoulder – a device that the famous showman Mollas claimed to have invented.

The show is usually accompanied by a small group of musicians and a singer, a great deal of shouting and noise and much witty dialogue

40

Greek shadow puppet of Karaghiosis

which keeps the audience in constant laughter. The plots of all the plays are familiar, so it is the topical cracks and impromptu repartee and continual involvement of Karaghiosis in schemes which are going to make his fortune but which invariably go wrong, that the people enjoy.

Between the wars the great showman of Karaghiosis was Mollas – a huge man with a voice to match. He would set up his screen in a partially demolished house fronting what we later would have described as a bomb site. Here tables and chairs for several hundred people would be set out and drinks brought from a nearby café. The performance began at 10.30 and went on till after one o'clock. Here is an extract from one of Jan's diaries (1938).

Behind the scenes were many minions – a young man with a guitar and several small boys were busy getting things ready for the Great Man . . . All round the walls were boxes and racks of figures and properties for their huge repertoire of shows . . . a wonderful ship with rigging most elaborately done and a sea serpent so huge that five people with rods were needed to work it. At the sides were racks for

41

figures to be used in this show . . . when all was ready and the audience (now full) was getting restive Mollas came in, very fat and sedate, resplendent in white. Someone at once passed him a special drink (for his throat), someone else switched the audience lights out and the theatre lights on, and the man with the guitar handed him his figure – Karaghiosis, and gave a sign to the orchestra.

Now began the Prologue – the same prologue is performed before every play. The orchestra blared out the most extraordinary rhythmic sound, fat Mollas nearly burst himself in a long high-pitched Arabic wail, working brilliantly two figures at once, and stamping rhythmically on the ground. There was a guitar solo in the middle while Mollas had another drink passed to him.

This went on for ten minutes. Often one heard the audience laugh, and there was great applause at the end. Then the lights were switched round, Mollas got another drink, and the scene was prepared for the play. . . Mollas spoke all the parts, changing his voice well and keeping up a constant flow of witticisms. They work to a definite story out of a repertoire of some fifty pieces, but the actual words are always impromptu, with many topical and political references and much vulgarity.

There was an occasional musical background by the orchestra, an occasional guitar solo and much battering of Karaghiosis. Also a lot of offstage scuffles in which everyone took part, jumping on the floor and shaking a bucket of broken glass. The audience loved it all . . . apparently Karaghiosis shows are considered only to be suitable for the lower classes, who come regularly.

Most of the manipulation was done by Mollas and very good it was. The guitarist took the secondary characters and when there were a large number of characters on the stage the little boys were allowed to hold them on the screen: but woe betide any of them who dared to attempt to make a gesture. Discipline was strong and punishment swift – a cuff on the neck from Mollas (who was probably also controlling two figures at the time!).

Nowadays the Karaghiosis theatre appears to be quite lively both in Greece and Cyprus and also in Paris where the well-known Greek painter C. Kyriazis also performs with the shadow puppets. But musicians seem to have become a thing of the past, having given way to the tape-recorder.

From Greece and Turkey the shadow puppets crossed Europe and had their moments of fame in Germany and Italy, Goethe having a shadow theatre built and helping to prepare the scripts for a performance, whilst the Italian Puppet Master, Ambroise, travelled around Europe presenting dramatic shadow performances with shipwrecks, violent storms, bridges crumbling into the waters and suchlike. But it was most of all in France, and particularly in Paris, that the shadow puppets enjoyed their greatest success, becoming a fashionable entertainment in cafés as well as theatres. Although called 'ombres chinoises' they were quite unlike the Chinese shows, the figures being made of stiff card or metal with none of the colour or lace-like perforations associated with the Chinese. In fact the French figures were just like the shadow profiles invented by Etienne de Silhouette as a cheap form of portraiture. The name most associated with this period in the shadow theatre was Seraphin. His small black figures were held against the screen by a 'handle' of cardboard from below, and movements of the jointed limbs were achieved by wires and strings. The piece for which he is most remembered is *The Broken Bridge*. This is still popular and played everywhere, including in Australia by Richard Bradshaw.

For about ten years at the end of the nineteenth century all Paris went to see the shadow plays of Henri Rivière at a cabaret called Le Chat Noir. The figures were moved in crowds, large masses and processions of people in dramatic attitudes were moved en bloc behind the screen by means of racks in which they slid. These racks were placed at different distances from the screen and the further they were from it the greyer, softer and mistier they appeared, giving an effect of perspective. These scenes of crowds or processions of people passing across the landscape were lit in a romantic and poetic way such as had never been seen before and created a strangely dream-like effect providing, as one writer has it '. . . a fantastic fairy-tale for the eye, deeply poetic in theme, of peculiar beauty in form, the whole a dream which vanished even as one strove to capture it'.

Nothing could be further from the down-to-earth shadow puppets of Greece and Turkey. In Paris it was a theatre of artists and poets, of designers and painters, and unfortunately it only lasted for about ten years and no one was able to follow Rivière. We have to wait thirty years for the next comparable figure to appear – Lotte Reiniger, who died in 1981 at the age of eighty-two. Her main work was of course done for the cinema – such marvellous creations as *The Adventures of Prince Achmed, Harlequin, Galathea, The Little Chimney Sweep* and many, many more. But even though she was making a stop-action film, Lotte Reiniger still manipulated every figure through every movement as if it was a dramatic performance. Each film required many thousands of frames; every limb of every figure had to be moved infinitesimally in

43

each frame. Her sense of timing was phenomenal and this, combined with her wit, her style and elegance and her great humanity, as well as her feeling for the dramatic, makes her work unique and quite unforgettable. We will look at more of it later.

In England, meanwhile, the Shadow Theatre had gone a very different way. It was probably first brought here from Italy and was called the 'Galantee' show from the Italian *galante* – fine or gallant; or the 'Chinese Shades' – a name brought back by sailors who had seen such shows in China. The English performers were Punch and Judy showmen who, when darkness fell, fixed a piece of calico across the proscenium of their booth and played with shadows by the light of candles. It must have been a hazardous occupation, for one showman quoted in *Mayhew's Characters* says:

'. . . when we are out performing we in generally burn three candles at once behind the curtain. One is of no utility, for it wants expansion don't you see. I don't like naphtha or oil lamps, 'cos we're confined there, and it's very unhealthy. It's very warm as it is, and you must have a eye like a hawk to watch it, or it won't throw the shadows. A brilliant light and a clean sheet is a great attraction, and it's the attraction is everything.'

Shadow puppets by Jan Bussell for *Thumbelina* by Hans Andersen as presented by The Hogarth Puppets

They seem to have had a wide selection of plays to offer as well as variety items. The showman quoted above lists *Kitty biling the Pot* or *The Wood-chopper's Frolic*, *Billy Button's Journey to Brentford on Horseback*, *Cobbler Johnson* and, of course, *The Broken Bridge*.

By the first part of the twentieth century in England, shadow puppets had almost disappeared. Doubtless many people were experimenting with them and entertaining their friends in homes and studios, but there were no shows for the general public to go to see and most people had never even heard of shadow puppets. In the late thirties we started to introduce shadow items in the middle of our Hogarth Puppets performances, sandwiched between two offerings by marionettes. We did this for several reasons. Firstly because we were interested in the shadows and wanted to experiment with them and develop our technique. Secondly, a full marionette performance is quite a strain on the audience who have to concentrate on a rather small stage area, and, as we presented the shadows above the opening of the marionette stage, the audience could take up a different posture both mentally and physically. Thirdly, shadow puppets are much smaller, lighter and more easily transported than marionettes, and when you are carting a puppet theatre around the world this is a serious consideration. Our first items were all short, comprising illustrations of sea shanties, short poems and comic cartoons, done entirely in black and white. We then tried a very simple Nativity play with coloured backgrounds behind black silhouettes, and spurred on by the success of this gave a version of Hans Andersen's story *The Beetle,* using coloured figures, coloured

Shadow puppets by Lotte Reiniger

backgrounds and simple scenery and props. These figures were all worked in the Greek style, with horizontal rods pressing the figures against the screen, which was of cotton sheeting.

In 1950 we persuaded Lotte Reiniger to design and cut for us all the scenery and figures for a version of Oscar Wilde's *The Happy Prince* using three screens, comprising some fifteen scene changes as the action moved from screen to screen, and a mass of figures, using a lot of colour as well as the basic and dramatic black silhouettes for which she was rightly so famous. She was a wonderful and inspiring person to work with, but also a very nerve-racking one as she never produced drawings or seemed to be working on a production at all – just 'thinking'. When we had already accepted a television engagement for *The Happy Prince* and were desperately needing to start rehearsals she said to us one day, 'Don't worry! It is all here! [pointing to her head] I vill just do so . . . and so . . . and it will be ver' good!' We went off to perform somewhere and on our return about twelve hours later she was sitting on the floor in a mass of cardboard snippings, and surrounded by all the exquisite scenes and figures we have loved performing with ever since. It was indeed 'ver' good!'

Since that time many people have taken to presenting shadow pup-

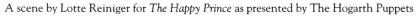

A scene by Lotte Reiniger for *The Happy Prince* as presented by The Hogarth Puppets

Shadow puppets by Richard Bradshaw – Super Kangaroo and friends (*photo: Michael Snelling*)

pets, and modern shows can be seen worldwide. One very popular player is Richard Bradshaw of Australia who performs all over the world with a fast moving, very witty and amusing cartoon-like show. It is a sophisticated and at the same time very Australian performance, and to travel with him through the outback countryside and watch him play to packed audiences of young Australians thoroughly enjoying the comedy inspired by the koalas, kangaroos, diggers, gum trees and aborigines of their daily life is a very enjoyable experience. Then to catch up with him in some European capital city and find the citizens there equally enraptured adds to the enjoyment.

Like everything nowadays the technique of the Shadow Puppet Theatre is leaping forward faster perhaps than its artistic content. But there are some very exciting things to be seen around at present, one of these certainly being *Gilgamesh*. This Italian production of the pre-Homer Babylonian myths is presented by Teatro Gioco Vita with designs by Emanuele Luzzati as a wild legendary tale for which they use giant shadows, growing and dissolving on a vast screen, making use of

47

Shadow puppets for *Gilgamesh* by Teatro Gioco Vita, Italy

several light sources to stage armies, battles and duels. Charioteers mow down the populace and gods and goddesses loom out of the firmament as the hidden manipulators move with choreographic precision to drama‑ tic musical accompaniment. The effect might almost be described as 'live cinema'. A far cry from the poetic, dreamlike processions so popular in Paris a hundred years ago; but this is theatre reflecting and commenting on its times.

Shadow puppets can also be used very successfully for a dramatic effect in a performance by other types of puppet. For instance, in a pro‑ duction of *Macbeth* done with marionettes we used the shadows of the three witches on a screen built into the set; in that way they could disap‑ pear instantly (at the touch of a light switch) causing Banquo to cry 'Whither are they vanished?'

In a production of *Bluebeard* we used a shadow puppet for a quite diffe‑ rent but equally successful effect. When Fatima calls 'Sister Anne! Sister Anne! Do you see anybody coming?' we light up a small shadow screen high up on the proscenium and there is the shadow of Sister Anne as if she is looking out of an upper window – or from the roof.

During a performance of glove and rod puppets given by the French company Les Roches, a bear sat down on the river bank and hung his tail in the water to catch a fish. A small shadow screen was revealed in the front of the booth and we saw the shadow of the bear's tail and the fish swimming around nibbling it, but refusing to be caught. There are many ways like this where a small shadow effect can greatly add to a production.

3

ROD PUPPETS

'They were all entwitched with your performance'
                                      Henryk Ryl of Poland

Basically rod puppets are simple to stage. All that is necessary is a
wooden or canvas 'wall' or screen above which the puppets appear and
behind which their manipulators are hidden. Once having got their
'wall', the puppeteers add all sorts of refinements to it – shelves and
hooks to hold properties, and a ledge across the top on which the puppets can put things down, or sit down on themselves.

It is also necessary to have tables either in front of or behind the
operators on which the puppets can be laid out ready and equipment
such as musical instruments or tape-recorders be easily to hand. The
puppets themselves can be very simple – just a head on a stick and two
swinging arms – or extremely elaborate with moving mouths and eyes,
joints to their fingers so that they can hold things or pick them up, complicated neck and waist joints etc.

The earliest rod puppets we know about are Javanese, called Wayang
Golek. These are three-dimensional, painted wooden puppets, dressed
in cotton batik. They are even more idol-like than the Wayang Kulit
and equally fascinating. Gorgeously decorated and gilded, they consist
of a head, about the size of a human fist, a torso to which the long-
skirted costume is attached, and delicate thin arms culminating in a
slender suggestion of hands, jointed at shoulder and elbow with fibre
cord. Like the flat leather Kulit figures they are worked by three rods.
The main rod, held inside the skirt, passes through the torso up to the
neck and the puppet turns its head as the rod is twisted. The other two
rods go to the hands and can be operated either singly or together. The
puppets appear over an opaque screen and the Dalang gives them very
lively and spirited movements, the arms swinging from side to side and
giving a real feeling of striding along. They can also have great dignity,

especially with the slow turning of the head, a movement we were told which has to be much practised. The characterisation of the different figures is easily conveyed to the initiated by the colouring of the face and especially the painting of the eyes, details of costume and headdress, as well as the angle at which the head is held upon the neck.

This type of puppet originated in west Java, though it may have come originally from India. As in all Javanese puppet shows there is a strong element of ancestor worship, initiation rites, and other primitive source material. In addition to the Ramayana and the Mahabharata plays, they perform the legends of Prince Menak, said to have been a forerunner of Mahomet as John the Baptist was of Jesus Christ. But these Islamic plays have never been so popular as the Hindu ones.

We have quite a collection of these beautiful figures. Some time ago we acquired two more in Holland. Although the heads were very fine, they had been smothered in a layer of thick brown paint, perhaps by someone who thought that as Indonesians have brown skins their puppets should be brown too. When all this paint had been carefully removed, disclosed beneath were about five layers of fascinating colour which had been overlaid, one upon the other, during what must have been the lives of several showmen. With the aid of books and pictures the figures were eventually restored, with their strange make-up indicating their characters, to how they must have looked to their first Dalang.

A group of Wayang Golek figures is fascinating to see – the Princes so reserved and elegant with their modest gait and downcast eyes; the Giants and monkey-like characters so bold with their crude features and fierce eyes gazing straight ahead. One feels not only how mysterious and outlandish they are, but how strange and foreign we must seem to them. When we demonstrate with two of these beautiful figures to audiences in England, we try to capture something of this feeling with the following lines, accompanied by Javanese gamelan music:

Two Princes of an ancient art,
Goleks of the Islamic Wayang,
By whom begotten
Like our names forgotten.
We wander on a foreign stage
Relics of another age,
Of Java's lost mythology a part.

Wayang Golek, round wooden rod puppets from Java

The Witches for *Macbeth* designed and made for The Hogarth Puppets production by Michael and Jane Eve

Men fashioned us in piety
Clothed in white and fasting as decreed,
As princes, gods and animals. Our rods
Controlling head and hand
We played the sagas of our land,
Of godly might and human frailty.
Through the ages without pity
New layers of colour thickened on each face.
Lost are our designs.
Clouded the outlines.
Revealed at last through stranger's hand
We gaze upon a foreign land,
Masked by meandering antiquity,
Masked by meandering antiquity.

A.H.

In the early years of this century the artist Richard Teschner, working in Austria, became fascinated with the Javanese rod puppets and developed a very beautiful and very elaborate theatre on their basic techniques. All the pictures one can see of his work, very well represented in many books and contemporary magazines, and the puppets themselves now in that part of the Hofburg, Vienna, which houses the Austrian theatre archives, are absolutely stunning. We saw him give a performance in London in 1934 and have to admit that this was a bitter disappointment. It was so slow and static, and the movements so repetitive that it was quite difficult to keep awake, concentrating on such a relatively small area. What one saw was extremely beautiful. We appeared to be looking at a circular window or mirror, the picture would fade out in some way, and when the lights again went up the scene had changed. It was all very lovely and artistic, but we longed for something theatrical to happen. It was Paul McPharlin, the American puppeteer and writer, who said, '. . . the eye of a camera sees them better than a spectator at a little distance. Therefore, to one who has been impressed by the figures in photographs they are disappointing in performance . . . Some of the plays are not good theatre.' But McPharlin added that the pictures of his work had been an inspiration to puppet workers the world over.

One such to be influenced both by Richard Teschner and the Javanese was the Russian, Nina Efimova, who started a puppet company with her husband, Ivan, in Moscow in the 1920s, playing Russian folk tales, a version of Macbeth and a play called The Banquet of Authors with life-size figures. She wrote a fascinating book, *The Adventures of a Russian Puppet Theatre,* which has been translated into English, and she was the first of the Russian puppet performers to make an impact on the rest of the world. We never saw her play, but her son once demonstrated Lady Macbeth for us. Some of her figures can now be seen in the Central State Puppet Theatre in Moscow.

Another Russian to be influenced by the Javanese and Efimova was Sergei Obrastzov. He studied the technique of the Golek puppets and saw their tremendous potentialities. He developed them unrecognisably, both by elaborating their jointing and mechanisation and also by using two or even more operators for one figure, so that there was practically no movement or series of movements they could not do. After becoming well known for his solo performances with glove puppets, Obrastzov founded the Central State Puppet Theatre in an old building in Moscow in 1931. He later moved to a marvellous opera house which he converted to combine two stages with workshops, restaurant, offices and museum as well as a training school. It is one of Moscow's show places and crowds gather outside it to watch the mechanical clock on the front strike the hours with a display of little

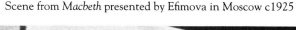

Scene from *Macbeth* presented by Efimova in Moscow c1925

Rod puppets in *Two Nil in Our Favour* by the Central State Puppet Theatre, Moscow

doors opening, figures appearing, bells ringing and on top of it all a magnificent animated cock. Obrastzov has a very large company of several hundred people and besides performances two or three times daily in their own building, they travel all over the world. We have seen them in many different countries besides Russia and the last time we caught up with them, in Sweden, they had added a new idea to the variety concert bill they were presenting. After an elaborate 'take-off' of a Spanish couple doing a Tango, the front screen was removed and the item performed again so that the audience could watch the five or six operators as they handled the two figures. Their own movements were as meticulously choreographed as those of the puppets, which we could now see they worked collectively, passing the rods from person to person as the figures moved through the exaggerated dance. It was a brilliant tour de force.

Another very amusing and clever show we saw once in Obrastzov's theatre in Moscow was *Don Juan*. Performed by rod puppets it gives a humorous revue-style look at the famous philanderer's romantic adventures as portrayed by different national theatrical styles – American, Japanese, Italian, Russian etc. No known language was used but an invented speech which sounded so like the tongue of each particular country in turn that we quite understood what was being conveyed by the speakers and felt that at any moment we would actually understand the words themselves.

Obrastzov and his Central State Puppet Theatre have had a tremendous influence everywhere in Eastern Europe, so that very large and talented companies are to be found in all these countries. The first big rod-puppet show we ever saw was in Poland in 1957. It absolutely bowled us over. The large proscenium opening was entirely filled with scenery and puppets. They were giving a play called *Zwyrtala the Old Musician* which tells how, when the old man dies, both Heaven and Hell claim him for their own. Zwyrtala arrives in Heaven, to the fury of the Devils down below – and all the bells of Heaven ring out! This was an unforgettable moment as the stage was filled with huge cut-out bells swinging to the peals. But the Old Musician causes so much distraction among the Angelic Host that he is finally returned to Earth for another spell of life.

At one point in the evening we were taken backstage where we were astonished as we watched a long line of girls, all carrying angels, emerge from the greenroom and take up their positions on stage. This was an absolute eye-opener to us. At that time our company numbered three or four and there was none larger in Britain. But this was not the only thing that amazed us. This puppet company in Warsaw employed the best de-

The Tango from *An Unusual Concert* by the Central State Puppet Theatre, Moscow

Rod puppets in *Zwyrtala the Old Musician* as presented by the Theatre Miniatura, Gdansk, Poland

signers, the best directors, musicians, authors and craftsmen to be found in Poland, and the necessary supporting staff as well. We had never dreamed of such riches. Many times since then we have played in East European countries and we are always asked the same questions, 'Who makes your puppets?' 'We do.' 'Who writes your plays?' 'We do.' 'Who drives your van?' 'We do.' 'Who builds your stage?' 'We do,' and so on and so on. Each party is amazed and a little envious of the other!

Gradually the rod techniques spread to Western Europe, the United States etc where, despite the more limited financial resources, some interesting things have been done. In fact there is a serious danger that the rod puppets will oust the more technically difficult marionettes worked by strings from above, and that the latter will cease to exist.

A company that owes nothing to Obrastzov, or indeed to Java, is the Hanneschen Rod Puppet Theatre in Cologne, founded in 1802. It is still highly successful even today and plays to a robust audience in their own local dialect. The material is often very topical and bawdy and is performed to a constant accompaniment of laughter from the public. We understood practically nothing that was said on any of the many occasions we witnessed performances, but the main story line was clear

Rod puppets from the Hanneschen Theatre, Cologne (*photo: Stadtbildstelle, Köln*)

and the mood of the audience infectious. The puppets are very large, about 76cm (30in) high, and supported between the legs by stout rods going right down to the floor. The bodies of the puppets are complete, the legs swinging free, and a good effect of walking and especially running can be achieved by a clever manipulator. One arm will often have a rod to it for gesturing or striking – very necessary in plays where blows are always being exchanged.

We spent our thirtieth wedding anniversary backstage at the Hanneschen, many drinks being exchanged in the interval! It was fascinating to be able to watch the manipulators who work in a sunken area so that they are completely hidden from the audience on the other side of the wooden barrier which separates them. It is a large area, perhaps 7·6m (25ft) square, with scenery representing Old Cologne hanging round it. The puppets are supported on racks on each side, waiting their entrances. There were about fifteen members of the company including stage staff, and everything was most efficiently and practically managed, all figures leaving the stage being immediately returned to their correct positions. The puppeteers speak the parts as they work, needing terrific voice and energy; and they must cover quite a lot of ground as they stride around, looking up at the figures they are operating above their heads. Everything is very realistically done and we watched with fascination as a large horse, centre stage, raised its tail in the air and 'did its business' – which was immediately hurried away and placed in the correctly labelled cupboard by a stage hand.

We were honoured by being asked to play ourselves in the Hanneschen Theatre, the first foreigners ever to do so. For this the sunken area had to be raised to bring our stage-level to a workable height – quite an elaborate undertaking. Although our performances are so very different from theirs, our marionettes so much smaller and more delicate than their robust rod puppets, and our humour much less noisy and knockabout, each company enjoyed and admired the work of the other, there being always a strong feeling of camaraderie – of brotherhood – between puppeteers, which rises above difficulties of language and even of idealogies.

In Paris about 1950 a young man called André Tahon founded a unique puppet company – Les Marottes. In medieval times the bauble which a Fool carried, and with which he teased the king and courtiers, was called a *marotte* in France. It consisted of a head upon a stick, ornamented usually with bells. André Tahon dispensed with the bells and added a costume and swinging arms. He then had a lively, simple

59

Compagnie des Marottes, Paris

puppet which by twisting and turning, posturing and posing was very
much alive. His next good idea was to realise that while one puppet
performing like this is good, two is even better, and four, six, eight,
even sixteen all in perfect unison are marvellous. Having achieved his
Chorus Line he then brilliantly imitated, parodied and outdid all the
dancing girls one has ever seen; American, Parisienne, Russian, Polish,

they came prancing on, singing in those shrill voices one has heard so often. They could change their costumes by simple duplication – they could pose in charming groups – they could play little scenes and if, for a change, they happened to be Mice – multiply themselves enormously in no time at all. Les Marottes and their compère Papotin, took the entertainment world by storm, playing everywhere and even achieving two Royal Command Performances in London. A success like this is very good for the Puppet Theatre, as a whole new public who would never set out to go to a puppet show, takes it in and enjoys it with the sort of entertainment it normally patronises.

When we started our show in 1932 we played only with marionettes, some time later adding shadow puppets, then glove puppets, but we didn't come to rod puppets for some thirty years or so. In 1968, however, we were asked by the Chief Librarian of Scunthorpe, the small steel-manufacturing town in Lincolnshire, to devise and carry out a course in puppetry for forty art teachers. This course was to run for about two weeks. The whole idea was a new venture for us. We decided immediately that we would aim at a performance of professional standard by the end of the period. All the students being art teachers, we knew they would be able to make puppets and paint scenery without difficulty. What they would most need to know would be what makes good entertainment with puppets, and how to achieve the effects they were aiming at. But above all we felt they would benefit from the sheer interest and excitement of all working together towards a final performance, and this certainly proved to be so.

We commissioned a play in blank verse from Michael Davies on the subject of Europa and the founding of Thebes. As the time allowed for preparation was so short we settled for narration and musical accompaniment pre-recorded on tape, and this meant the students were able to start rehearsals the very first day as there was no need to wait till they knew their lines. It is of course impossible for puppeteers – unlike actors – to rehearse carrying a script around, as their hands and eyes are fully occupied with the puppets they are working. We planned all the basic necessities for making the puppets in advance. Michael Eve designed very bold heads and hands which could be cut out of thin cardboard, as well as the very elaborate scenery. We made wooden shoulder-pieces from which the simple costumes could hang, and for which we dyed yards and yards of cotton material in different colours. Everything we could think of in the way of rods for manipulating, for arm sections or for necks, screw-eyes, wire for jointing etc, was assembled along with

Backstage view at Scunthorpe during rehearsal of *Europa* (*photo: N. Reeder*)

wood, canvas, and paint for the scenery. We had planned a production on three levels, one above the other. The front two levels were for the mortal puppets and the back one – the highest – was where the gods and goddesses appeared. The lowest row of scenery acted as a screen to mask the puppeteers working behind it. The two others were raised up on legs. The operators behind the first row walked on the floor, the next were raised up on a platform about 45cm (18in) high and at the back the puppeteers had to stand on step-ladders to work the gods amongst the clouds. The scenery could be changed at all levels by running in different ground rows. At times the front level became the sea complete with ships, whales and the god Poseidon.

All the making and rehearsing of this major opus took place in the very nice little theatre in Scunthorpe where the final performance was to be given. We literally took it over and the whole building hummed with activity. People passing by in the street stood in amazement watching the students working in the foyer, the box office, and every available inch of space. A tremendous excitement was engendered. As well as making and painting we rehearsed for some time every day from the very beginning, the students holding up rods to indicate their puppet at the first session, and these rods gradually acquiring heads, hands, costumes etc as time passed. Everyone worked incredibly hard, we had positively to drive them home at about midnight, only to find some hard at it again by 7.30 next morning. Wives, husbands, girl friends, all had to take a back seat for those two weeks. Some retaliated by joining in the proceedings and giving a hand with the making and painting.

For the one and only performance there was a full house. All went very well and there was great enthusiasm. Everyone said they felt expanded and stretched and some of them formed a group of their own and planned further productions. We corresponded with them for some years, but then as always happens in the theatre, we lost touch with all those marvellous students, as we and they moved on to other things. We only hope they benefited from all their hard work and devotion.

As we have said before, one of the hazards of playing with puppets in theatres with audiences in circles and balconies, is that the manipulators' heads become visible. Henryk Ryl of the Arlekin Puppet Theatre, at Lodz in Poland, overcame this problem in one production by having the entire stage floor (normally non-existent for rod puppets) consist of wooden isosceles triangles of about 30cm (12in) base, supported by uprights on heavy stands, forming a ceiling over the heads of the puppeteers. Around each triangle of floor a space of about 5cm (2in) was left for the puppets' rods. In rehearsal the operators had to learn by which triangle they should take up position, and by what route they should arrive there. At first they hated it and regarded it as a loss of liberty. But they soon became accustomed to it and learned to appreciate the discipline – or so Henryk told us!

A quite different type of rod puppet which we found very useful as an opening number, particularly to grasp the attention of audiences composed of older children who can be restless at being taken to see what they are afraid is 'kid's stuff', we called *The Wooden Eyes*. This act consists of two large Eyes which can open, shut, and swivel, accompanied by a very mobile Mouth, all worked by thin black rods (umbrella spokes actually), which appear quite disembodied above the puppet stage. We found even the most sceptical teenagers were interested in these – gave us their immediate attention – and settled down to enjoy the rest of the performance.

63

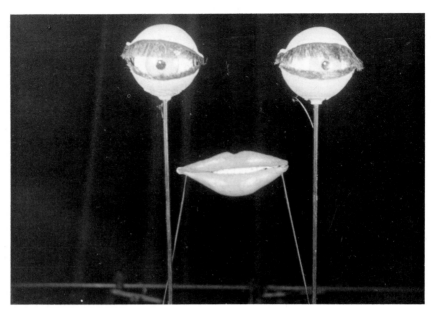
Wooden Eyes by The Hogarth Puppets

The Eyes and Mouth were accompanied by the following verse:

The Theatre of the Wooden Eyes.
Eyes made of Wood – but not so blind!
Through us a new perspective find.
Open wide your own two optics,
See the sense behind our antics.
Tell good from bad, tell truth from lies,
In the theatre of the Wooden Eyes.
Pleading Eyes! Roving Eyes! Smiling Eyes! Cross Eyes!
Searching Eyes! Sleepy Eyes! Surprise! Surprise!
We need a Mouth that we may speak.
We need no tongue – that's in our cheek!
[Mouth appears, laughs, yawns, giggles]
Ring Up The Curtain!

A.H.

An exciting personality who appeared in the puppet world was Fred Schneckenburger from Frauenfeld in Switzerland. He was a cultured businessman interested in all the arts and, at the time we knew him, particularly in puppets. His work was very socially and politically con-scious, and his figures were always surrealist. When we first saw them in

1950 they were considered shockingly avant garde by many puppeteers. There was the Bandit, all of whose fingers were revolvers; the Politician, whose head split in two allowing a small bubble to emerge; the Journalist with wide-open mouth lined with newsprint; and among many others and perhaps the most moving puppet we have ever seen, the Returned Soldier, whose wounded face was so terrible no one could bear to look at him and he wandered solitary.

All Schneckenburger's plays conveyed a message and he had no place in his repertoire for merely pretty, nostalgic or sentimental acts. We remember how distressed he was at the Polish Puppet Theatre's use of what had been 'work' songs, merely as effective entertainment, complaining that the sufferings and struggles of the peasants who had originally sung these songs had been completely forgotten – or hidden.

There is an enormous number of State Puppet Theatres to be found in

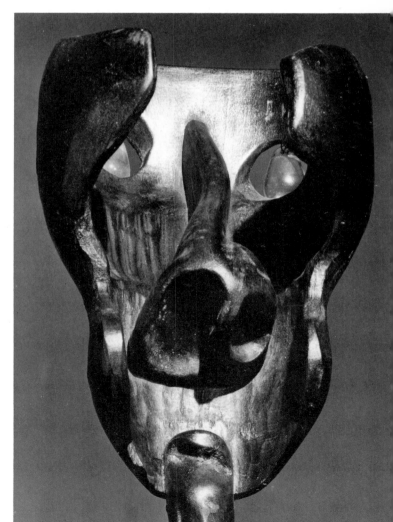

Puppet for *Cabaret* by
Fred Schneckenburger,
Switzerland

Eastern Europe, mostly using rod puppets, and we have spent happy hours in many of them. Apart from those in Russia and Poland already mentioned there is the marvellous theatre, originally called The Cave of Tales, in Budapest, directed by Dezso Szilagyi. They have appeared in England bringing with them a particularly fine production of *Petrushka* to Stravinsky's music. In Bucharest at the Tsandarica Theatre, directed by Margareta Niculescu, we had our first experience of what can be achieved with a large dedicated company using many different kinds of puppet and with top designers and sculptors and specially commissioned music and plays. It was a revelation! We ourselves played in the Tsandarica and met with enormous kindness and friendliness, our working smocks being snatched away and returned freshly laundered and with flowers pinned to the lapels! From the Bulgarian Puppet Theatre in Sofia we remember with particular pleasure the magnificent and highly original production of *Krali Marco,* the legendary hero who defended his people against the Turks. Once again we saw what the Puppet Theatre can do when top artists are at its disposal. With another puppet theatre in Bulgaria – that in Gabrova – we exchanged puppets. We sent them a replica of our rubber-headed clown Rufus, and they sent us a very large rod puppet – the Boy from the play *The Boy and the Wind* by Nina Trendafilova.

We have to admit that for us personally the rod puppet is the one we tend to use least, although there are productions for which it is the most suitable. For a small company they do not have the tremendous advantage of the glove puppet that one showman can handle two puppets at a time.

Marionettes are undoubtedly superior to rod and glove puppets in being complete with legs and feet, and they can be shown in most buildings without difficulty. They are also the ones that the public most like to see. Rod puppets often appear to us to be presented in a very two-dimensional manner, using a wide proscenium in which they tend to move from side to side rather than around a whole area. But they do have one tremendous advantage – they are comparatively simple to work. Any good actor can perform with rod puppets. After a few minutes' practice the basic technique of a simple puppet is acquired and the operator has then only to transfer his own movements to the puppet; though he needs skilful direction from the front to ensure that what he thinks he is making the puppet do, as he looks up at it from below, is actually what the audience sees looking at it from out in front. This technical simplicity means that there is no great difficulty in finding manipulators; training in acting and directing is more important with rod puppets than training in manipulation. Marionettes, on the other hand, are technically very difficult to work well and it requires a long period of practice and training to create a manipulator. Most actors prefer to appear themselves on the stage rather than undergo long training and then become virtually invisible to an audience, but it is possible for an actor to work as a rod-puppet manipulator for periods when he is out of work on the stage. These are some of the factors which are tending to make the marionette a rarer bird to find and there is a real danger that it may die out altogether.

Realising this some years ago, Henryk Ryl invited us in 1970 to take our marionette theatre to Poland and play in five different cities – Warsaw, Lodz, Wroclaw, Torun and Lublin – in an attempt to popularise puppets worked by strings. We played to the general public, but included in our audiences were large numbers of performers who normally played with rod puppets in the various State Puppet Theatres. After each performance the professional puppeteers would stay behind and talk. They were intrigued and interested, asked many questions, tried their hands at working the marionettes and appeared genuinely impressed. Henryk Ryl – a great communicator in any language – said, 'They are all entwitched with your performance!' But so far as we have been able to find out, they then all went on performing with their rod puppets.

4

MARIONETTES

'Give me a handful of strings and I will make a puppet live!'
Italian Showman

The derivation of the word 'marionette' is not certain, but may well be from the diminutive of Mary given to the figure of the Virgin in the Nativity scenes displayed at Christmas. This idea is strengthened by the fact that such figures were sold in the Rue des Marionettes in Paris for many years, although this street has now ceased to exist. Another theory is that these puppets were brought to France in the reign of Charles IX by an Italian called Marion, and after whom they were named. We shall never know!

As we have already said, puppets worked by strings from above are the most sophisticated and complicated to manipulate. The equipment needed to display them is heavy, bulky and difficult to transport, and takes longer to assemble and dismantle before and after a performance than that of other types of puppet. We are talking here of a large full-scale marionette theatre, with proscenium, 'bridges' for the puppeteers etc. Unless playing in a theatre with a raked auditorium with very good sightlines, the puppets must be raised up to a considerable height over stage level, say 60 or 90cm (2 or 3ft). And the puppet operators will need to stand on at least the same level, and often very much higher. Even with modern materials, platforms strong enough to bear several operators need to be pretty substantial. To hide these manipulators a proscenium screen is necessary, as well as a backcloth, and this must be strong and firm standing. Add lighting, scenery, sound equipment and a large rack on which the puppets can hang whilst awaiting their entrances – for marionettes cannot be left lying down on floor or table

A nineteenth-century Burmese Prince and Princess

Figures for *Kinuta*, a Japanese Noh play, made for Roel Puppets by Gerald Shaw c1930

like their rod, glove or shadow counterparts – and you can readily see why many showmen fight shy of performing with marionettes and settle for the other forms of puppet.

For the amateur setting up a puppet theatre in his own house it is much simpler (see Fig 7). A firm table to stand on placed behind a low stage with scenery to mask the operator's legs; a proscenium screen with an opening cut in it standing on the front edge of the stage and a rack behind for the puppets to hang from are not difficult to make; and if it can be left permanently in position so much the better. But for a large, professional touring company it is a very different matter. If playing in theatres large puppets must be used, and that means the 'bridges' must be raised well above stage level, probably above the level of the puppets' heads. If the production is an elaborate one several 'bridges' may be needed, allowing for scenery to stand beneath them and for the operators to move from one to the other, giving the puppets freedom to occupy the whole acting area.

The strings of marionettes are fixed to a wooden cross known as the 'control' or 'perch'. From this latter word the rack on which the puppets hang is called the 'perchery'. The strings should be 'tuned' so that the figure is always completely balanced when at rest, and the slightest movement of the control should invoke a corresponding movement in the puppet below. People have tried various other ways of controlling marionettes. The Burmese, for instance, have loops of string going from one side of the puppet's body to the other, from one side of the head to the other, from leg to leg, from shoulder to shoulder, arm to arm. These loops of strings are all hung over the operator's arm between the elbow and wrist, and the other hand gathers up and pulls individual strings. Olive Blackham, the distinguished British puppeteer, experimented with the strings of a puppet attached to the fingertips of a pair of gloves. She operated her puppet of The Woman in Kreymborg's *Lima Beans* in this manner. Like the Burmese, this method of manipulation suffers from the difficulty of picking up or putting down a puppet quickly. This would not be so important in a State Puppet Theatre where there are usually large numbers of manipulators available, but it can be fatal in a small company where people have to move rapidly from figure to figure.

Marionettes have been around a long time. Jointed figures have been found in Egyptian tombs as well as in Greek and Italian excavations, and there are references to controlling figures by strings in the writings of Aristotle, Marcus Aurelius and others; but experts are still arguing as to what exactly these references mean. Do they refer to puppets as we

Head of an Old English Marionette (*The Hogarth Collection*)

think of them or would they be nearer to automata? This is another imponderable to which we shall probably never have the answer. By the Middle Ages, references are obviously to puppets, though we can still not be sure how they were operated or what plays they gave for the details that devoted researchers have unearthed are not very informative. A charming, though completely negative titbit in Paul McPharlin's *Puppet Theatre in America* quotes a document referring to a Mexican puppet show in 1569 'which would give the gentry no call to blush!'

Even much later, in references to puppets in eighteenth-century England for instance, it is often difficult to decide what types are being used. The famous puppet showman Martin Powell, who performed for several years around the time of Queen Anne both in Bath and in Covent Garden, London, almost certainly used marionettes supported by a stiff wire to the head, with the addition of strings for other limbs and movements. But it is very possible that he also used glove puppets, lay figures and even large wooden cut-outs as supporting casts. The list of his plays is formidable, including a version of *Faust, The Age of Innocence and The Fall of Man*, the *Second Tale of a Tub, The Blind Beggar of Bethnal Green* and Ben Jonson's *Bartholomew Fair*. Some of his greatest successes were with parodies of currently playing operas. Shakespeare was also performed. Samuel Johnson is reported to have said that *Macbeth* was much more impressive with puppets than with actors.

72

When the live theatre was in disfavour, and at one period even banned in London, the puppet theatres thrived and drew the crowds wherever they performed. It was even said that the showmen in Covent Garden used the sound of the church bells as a signal that their show was about to begin, so depriving the clergy of their congregations and decimating their offertories. Perhaps it is from this period that the human actor's traditional and instinctive dislike of puppets stems.

By the twentieth century the heyday of the Puppet Theatre seems to have been over, certainly in England. The large marionette companies were breaking up and performances were to be found only in fairgrounds or as music-hall turns. There had been many large and famous companies amongst them, travelling all over the British Isles and undertaking enormous journeys abroad. Some of these companies spanned over a hundred years, passing down the generations, their names becoming household words. In the early 1950s we were visited backstage by a Miss Holden, a venerable lady who reminisced about the great days when her family had toured all over Europe, America and Great Britain. They travelled a very large fit-up which they used to set up on the stage inside a tent to guard their secrets. She also insisted her father used to employ local midgets to walk out of the stage door as the audience was leaving and that she had heard people saying 'Look! There are the puppets going home!'

By the end of World War I, audiences were becoming more sophisticated and the days of these large companies were numbered. An exception to this was the Teatro Dei Piccoli of Rome, founded and directed by the remarkable Italian, Vittorio Podrecca. From 1913 onwards this amazing company travelled to all the great cities of the world, performing scaled-down operas, fairy tales, lavish spectacles of all kinds, together with clever variety acts. All was presented in the most stylish and romantic manner imaginable. For thirty or forty years they were without rival anywhere in the world.

In England, meanwhile, where the indigenous Puppet Theatre had more or less ceased to exist, there was awakening of interest in the mid-1920s. As a result of the publication of a book *Everybody's Theatre* by H. W. Whanslaw, a group of enthusiasts met together and founded the British Model Theatre Guild, which still exists, with the word 'Puppet' added to its title. At the same time serious work with marionettes was being done by such artists as William Simmonds, the woodcarver, and Olive Blackham who founded the Roel Puppets. For several years Simmonds gave a short season annually in a small theatre in London with

73

Caveman – a puppet made by
Stanley Maile c1928 (*The Hogarth
Collection*)

his delightful carved wooden figures of fauns, centaurs, nymphs and
shepherds, which he manipulated entirely alone – a figure in each hand
– on a curved stage, singing and speaking for the figures himself, or
accompanied by his wife on the virginals.

Olive Blackham, working in the Cotswolds, was also experimenting
with marionettes, many of them great heavy figures of extraordinary
power, performing Morality Plays, Japanese Noh Plays, Edward Lear
etc. We have some of these figures in our collection, and even when
they are hanging still and mute on the perchery they have a personality
and dramatic force which is quite extraordinary.

But the marionettes had lost their former public and had to struggle to
find a new one. The cinema was everybody's entertainment now, even
in the remoter parts of the country. Neither the intelligentsia nor the
hoi polloi felt the need to see puppet shows, which had to retreat from
the theatres and find a meagre public in village halls, upper rooms over
restaurants, private houses and large stores at Christmas time. The
London Marionette Theatre of Waldo Lanchester and H. W.
Whanslaw gave performances in a small studio in Hammersmith and

our Hogarth Puppets, with no permanent theatre, led a wandering existence with the show piled high on an old car and a tent as a home. In those days farmers would always let one camp in a field and their wives were generous with eggs, milk, cream etc. The local church hall could be hired from the parson – so long as it wasn't Lent, when the poor puppet player was expected to fast indeed! It was quite a romantic life, though a hard one; and we learnt to cope with almost every situation – booking halls, putting up publicity notices on trees and telegraph poles, selling tickets, dealing with audiences, managing with candles when there was no electricity and finally shooing off the cows as we counted the takings over cocoa back at the tent.

Marionettes in *Richard III* by Ralph Chessé, California, USA

Conditions in the Puppet Theatre were much the same all over the world. But television was just around the corner and that was to give back to the marionettes a place with the public, though sadly it was not the robust, popular public of the eighteenth and nineteenth centuries, nor the public that had flocked to Podrecca's marionette operas. It was a fickle, unseen mass audience which tended over the years to get younger and younger, until this year it was reported that the average age at a puppet festival in Plymouth was three years old! So are the mighty fallen.

But only temporarily, for there are now many puppet companies who have made a place and name for themselves both in their home countries and travelling abroad. They have adapted their shows to the changing times and audiences, they have learned from cartoon films and the political commentators, and new materials allow them to make puppets quickly so that they can change the content of their programmes rapidly and keep up to date. More and more small towns have theatres and community centres where they can play, travelling is much easier between and within countries, and all sorts of inventions and improvements in lighting and sound are now available and being taken full advantage of by the puppeteers.

The Salzburg Marionette Theatre was founded in 1913 by Anton Aicher, specialising in Mozart operas with singers who sat in the pit with the orchestra and sang for the puppets. As well as playing every year in its home city, the company has travelled to many countries and has a band of admiring followers wherever it goes. We have seen them in a Court Theatre in Munich, in Sadler's Wells Theatre, London, in Bath, in Windsor and in a small village hall in Germany, where the oxen could be heard stamping and snorting in the barn adjoining. In this rustic setting the local audience derived as much pleasure from *Il Seraglio* as did their more sophisticated counterparts in capital cities. It is not only that the combination of Mozart opera and marionettes has great appeal, but that the Salzburg Marionettes strive for and usually achieve perfection – no less. No pains are spared, training and rehearsal are rigorous and take many months, the puppets are beautifully made and dressed, and it is said that the operators even have to learn to breathe like the singers the puppets are representing, before the production is considered ready to set before the public. Whether Mozart operas are the ideal vehicle for puppets is an arguable point, but the Salzburg Marionettes perform so perfectly, the settings are so beautiful, the singing of such a high standard, that one is compelled to set aside any reservations and just enjoy it all.

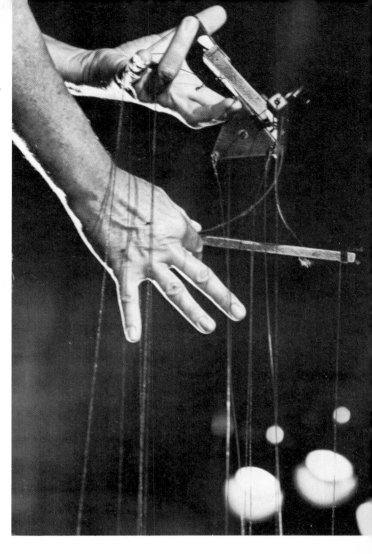

The hands of a manipulator
of a Salzburg marionette

A very different marionette theatre is the Spejbl and Hurvinek Company founded by Professor Josef Skupa in Pilsen in Czechoslovakia, and which now has its own theatre in Prague. The character of Spejbl, the father, was designed by Skupa and carved by Karel Nosek in 1920. Six years later a son, Hurvinek, was carved by Gustav Nosek and a great partnership was born. Until his final illness Professor Skupa spoke the dialogue for both puppets and manipulated Spejbl, while his wife, Irina, manipulated Hurvinek. Around this father and son act, which would give two or three dialogues of topical satire during the evening, a marvellous variety of other acts was performed. There was the Orchestra with its romantic conductor, swaying and swooping at the most

Professor Skupa's famous puppets Hurvinek and Spejbl, Prague

impossible angles; the Village Band, thumping, tooting and scraping its way through its familiar pieces, each puppet so strongly dilineated, both in carving and in manipulation that you felt you had known them all your life. And there was the Choir – tremendously caricatured, familiar types, whose jaws would almost dislocate as they gave their utmost to each song. Once or twice in the course of an evening a soft, even sentimental, act was introduced, coming almost as a relief from the constant ripple of amusement and shouts of laughter that most of the programme called forth. The company consisted of twelve or so people and we got to know them well, they were so friendly and helpful. We played in their Prague theatre in 1948, an unforgettable experience, both harrowing and rewarding; the former because it was at the time of the Communist take-over and everyone was aware that a curtain was coming down between the two halves of Europe, and rewarding because we had a marvellous reception from the audience and felt we were really at home among friends with the puppeteers backstage. We had one real problem – they shook our hands so often and crushed them so warmly that we were afraid they would be too bruised to manipulate the puppets, and were constrained to walk about holding them behind our backs.

Skupa was not only a great puppeteer, but a great man and much loved by his countrymen. When the Nazis occupied Pilsen he was imprisoned for the liberal views his puppets expressed on the stage, and his house was ransacked. Some children found the figures of Hurvinek and Spejbl thrown on a rubbish heap, recognised them, saved them, and returned them to Skupa when he was released. In later years we once expressed surprise at some anti-government stance he took. He looked at us proudly and said, 'Skupa is Skupa!' His theatre still continues and his two famous puppets still perform, adapting themselves to changing tastes. It was a unique creation.

In 1946 the English puppet community was glad to welcome John Wright who came from South Africa to settle here, providing not only employment and training but inspiration to young puppeteers ever since. He is living proof that if you want something badly enough and are determined enough, you will get it. Meeting him walking along Oxford Street not long after his arrival, we asked him what his plans were. 'I shall find a studio in Hampstead,' he replied. We laughed at this.

Pondo characters carved in wood by John Wright for *The Honeybird*, a play based on an African legend (*photo: Derek Beck*)

'He's got a hope,' we thought – practically everyone we knew was look-ing for a studio at that time. But John Wright knows what he wants and sets vibrations to work so that he gets it. Sure enough, shortly afterwards he was installed and working in a Hampstead studio. To us, still emerg-ing from the drabness of wartime London, his whole set-up seemed very glamorous, and still carried around it a feeling of sunshine and warmth and gaiety. The girls were very pretty and dashing and would appear with laburnum blossoms hanging from their ears. They definitely brightened up the English puppet scene. He also broadened our horizons with his beautifully carved and stylish puppets. In more recent years, since he and his wife Lyndie founded the Little Angel Theatre in Islington, their productions of Menotti's *Amahl and the Night Visitors* and Stravinsky's *The Soldier's Tale* have been landmarks in British puppetry. If his com-pany has not had the resources to achieve the perfection of the Salzburg Marionettes, the Little Angel is certainly a centre where talented and enthusiastic puppeteers can meet and work and talk and develop their ideas, and perhaps gradually push forward the artistic frontiers in a

Barry Smith Theatre of Puppets; The Duchess Grognon about to be swallowed by Envy from *The Crystal Palace* by J. R. Planche

country which is still largely philistine in its attitude towards puppet theatres. And that is certainly an asset in any country.

Using all the different types of puppet, Barry Smith's Theatre of Puppets also exerts a considerable influence on the puppet scene. No two of his productions ever follow the same lines; he is always experimenting with his puppets, his material and his methods of presentation, so that it is quite difficult to keep up with him. A production is more than likely to have been scrapped, however successful, before one gets around to going to see it. His early programmes of short, satirical items, mostly with rod and glove puppets, were always interesting, and he had an outstanding production of the Victorian pantomime *The Crystal Palace* by J. R. Planche. He gives a very good performance with Punch and Judy in his evening on the history of Punch; and when you add *Faust*, Boccaccio and forays into Beckett it is plain what a fertile mind he has, never playing safe with something he knows is successful, but always adventuring into fresh fields. He is often called on to advise and assist when puppets are needed in productions of stage plays and this work must be a marvellous inspiration and source of new ideas, something he never shows signs of running out of.

The variety of the French Puppet Theatre over the years has always been a source of admiration if not envy on this side of the Channel. There are many regional characters still to be found there today, something unknown in Britain. Parks in large cities often have their permanent puppet theatres for children, and there always seems to be a stream of clever and amusing companies springing up to perform in nightclubs, cabaret, television etc. One of the regional characters, Lafleur of Amiens, has recently had a statue erected to him by public subscription. There are no longer the big touring companies of marionettes that were around at one time, in fact the puppet worked by strings is not often seen in France today and most of the spirited and much admired figures now gaze at us sadly from their glass cases in museums. One famous company was Les Waltons or Pajot-Waltons as they were sometimes known, a family affair which lasted for 140 years. In *Comoedia* of 22 March 1935, Gaston Baty has left a vivid account of this company's history from the time of Napoleon until 1939. We met the last two members – a brother and sister – of this family of puppeteers in Charleville in the Ardennes in 1961, where we enjoyed their lively and amusing company. In 1962 marvellous photographs of them appeared in *J'aime les Marionettes* by Jean Mohr, showing the Walton puppets, sad, shabby but dignified and moving as ever, stowed in a garage near Paris. Where are they now? We

Lafleur, the puppet character from the Ches Cabotans Company of Amiens, France

have heard no more. There is something almost tragic about puppets left behind and not needed again. They give an impression of life suspended, animation suddenly cut off. Their masters die and vanish but the puppets are left hanging, motionless, awaiting a controlling hand. This was most forcefully brought home to us by an old French showman who gave us a much used but discarded puppet, and when we told him we would use it in our show cried out, with tears in his eyes, 'Our puppet will dance again!'

In 1936 a considerable stir, almost a revolution, was caused in the puppet world by the appearance of Bob Bromley from America in nightclubs and music halls without any form of staging or proscenium. He simply stood there, with a spotlight focussed on the puppets and worked his large marionettes, one after the other in full view of the audience – dressed in a dinner jacket! Such a thing had never been seen before and the public loved it. His appearance and personality definitely added to the appeal of his acts and from then on he was in demand everywhere that mattered – Royal Command Performances at the London Palladium, Grace Kelly's wedding in Monaco, the Cirque Medrano in Paris, the Hilton Ice Show, nightclubs, cabarets, television. Even standing there before the public with no concealment, no scenery, just himself and a rack of four or five puppets, he made each character a personality, with a life of its own separate from its manipulator. This wasn't just cleverness, it was creativity as he presented the Sad Clown with the burst balloon, the Striptease Dancer, Trapeze Acrobat, portraits of film stars and so on. We met up with him in a TV studio in Alexandra Palace in 1946. The programme was a mixed bag of puppet acts of several puppeteers and Bob, who was appearing at the Palladium at the time, gallantly agreed to bring a figure along and perform with it. But Equity

Bob Bromley with clown and balloon in 1955 (*photo: Almasy*)

stepped in and wouldn't allow him to appear. Not in the least disgruntled or put out he simply handed the large Dissecting Skeleton he had brought to me, showed me how the control worked and allowed me to work it before the TV cameras – a generosity of spirit which we still recall with admiration.

Two other Americans who used to appear on the variety scene frequently, were the double act Walton and O'Rourke, who became known in addition for providing and manipulating the important and attractive puppets in the film *Lili*, with Leslie Caron and Mel Ferrer. One of the difficulties of successful puppeteers is that if they are always performing they have no time to make new figures and renew their acts. Walton and O'Rourke told us that they solved this problem by making their large papier-mâché figures in the washbasins of their hotel bedrooms. They must have been very popular guests, as anyone who has had to clear up the mess made with papier-mâché can testify! According to Paul McPharlin in his *Puppet Theatre in America,* Walton and O'Rourke made their first appearance in a huge bottle advertising beer! They made so much money at this that it set them on the road to fame and fortune.

An American Puppet Master well known in his own country, but who gained an enormous worldwide audience through a film, is Bil Baird of New York, who was responsible for the puppet sequence in *The Sound of Music* with Julie Andrews. A very talented and original puppeteer, he also sees himself as a citizen of the world much more than many of his countrymen. With his wife, Cora, and a large company, he played in India, Afghanistan, Russia and other countries. He was for some years a member of the council of UNIMA (Union Internationale de la Marionette), the world puppet organisation, and attended its conferences in many countries. Unfortunately, except for *The Sound of Music* we never saw a show by his theatre, but his puppets appear always to have a great vitality, are very much caricatures and set out to comment on the human race with all its peculiarities and imperfections. He seems to have done literally everything possible with puppets, from delicate, sensitive, carved wooden figures to huge larger-than-life creations for advertising in such venues as the Chicago World Fair. Over many years we have found his very idiosyncratic Christmas cards a delight, and once watched during an interminable lunch in Bratislava as he whiled away the endless waits between courses, drawing in crayon on his plate a most decorative and appetising meal of fish, which was reverentially carried away by the waiter. Perhaps it still exists today, behind glass in a case.

Puppet by Albrecht Roser, Germany

As one would expect of a country which abounds in legends, gnomes, dark pine forests etc, and with a terrain and climate which, until recently, ensured that many areas were cut off and isolated in wintertime causing the inhabitants to turn to home entertainment, Germany has a long history of Puppet Theatre, and houses the world's most famous and comprehensive puppet museum in the Puppentheatersammlung in Munich. Marionettes in Germany have tended to be rather large and ponderous, and for many years seemed to present a solid diet of fairy tales and *Faust,* performing the macabre rather than the light fantastic. An exception to this trend is provided by the work of Albrecht Roser from Stuttgart, whose original approach to the Puppet Theatre has brought him recognition all over Europe as well as in America, Australia and Japan. He works in full view of the audience, with the assistance of a girl who remains mostly in the background attending to lights, music, effects etc, and only occasionally helps with the puppets. Roser works on a slightly raised rostrum several feet square at the back of which hang rows of puppets, for he gives a full evening's entertainment and not just the twelve- or fifteen-minute acts of the variety performers. His show is intended for adult audiences. It consists of many short items, perhaps fourteen or fifteen in an evening, with one or two characters – such as his clown Gustaf – reappearing during the course of the programme. Although he makes many of his figures himself he has some most attractive characters carved for him by Herbert Bross, who was a skilled craftsman and a great innovator and experimenter with different types of jointing, controlling, stringing etc. Roser's programme is very varied, at times witty, at times robustly comic, sometimes sad or even macabre. His boldly drawn characters are brilliantly manipulated, every puppet in every sketch fully developed, nothing left to chance. He is like the Salzburgers in this. Watching him one never feels 'Oh, that didn't quite come off!' or 'I wonder if he really intended that.' The audience feels absolutely secure in his hands, relaxes and enjoys itself. There is also so much to see, to hear and to think about, that Roser's performance of *Gustaf und sein Ensemble* as he entitles it, can be seen over and over again with added enjoyment each time.

Looking at the puppet scene in various European countries it is interesting to find that in many of them there are local marionette characters – regional heroes or celebrities perhaps – which exist to this day, still performing even though the communities which they sprang from have been absorbed into the national life and no longer have the strong regional identity they had before travel became easy, distances shrank and television made the whole world one.

A most interesting survivor from the past is the Toone Theatre in Brussels, situated down a narrow passage, the Impasse Schuddeveld, just off the Grande Place. No one knows how many centuries this theatre has been in existence, all records prior to 1812 being lost. Before that date all is rumour, folk legend and folk memory. 'Toone' is apparently a corruption of 'Antoine', and is the title by which each successive 'Master of the Puppets' has been known; 1812 saw the accession of Toone I who reigned until 1865, Toone II stayed until 1890 and so on. The present incumbent is Toone VII, in normal life M. José Géal. Toone marionettes are very large, 90 to 120cm (3 to 4ft) in height, and each is operated by two stiff wires, one to the head and one to the right arm. A great deal of duelling and fighting is a feature of the productions and the repertoire includes such dramas as *Les Quatre Fils Aymon*, *Faust*, *The Temptation of St Antony*, *Macbeth* and *Carmen*. An old invitation card exists for a gala performance in the middle of the nineteenth cen-

Boy from the play *The Boy and the Wind* made by the State Puppet Theatre of Gabrova, Bulgaria

tury when the audience was promised 'A grand drama in five Acts and twenty-seven tableaux, with two Duels, one Transformation, three Assassinations and seven Changes of Scenery'. At this same period the spectators were being warned not throw fruit peel on pain of being 'flung through the door'.

Nothing was thrown when we saw a performance of *Othello* there, and it was a fascinating evening. Throughout the show the head and shoulders of Toone himself, wearing a traditional checked cloth cap, is visible to the audience in a window by the side of the stage. He speaks for all the characters during the whole performance, changing his voice as necessary for each, male and female – a remarkable feat. What is more he plays either in French or in Flemish according to the requirements of the audience. If they are predominantly French, Toone speaks French that night. If there is a large party of Flemish speakers, as on the night we were there, Toone performs in Flemish. The language it is true is simple, not exactly Shakespeare, just what is necessary to develop the character and put the plot over, and there is a great deal of crude humour and knockabout comedy. But when Othello had killed Desdemona there was suddenly a moment of real tragedy as he realised what he had done and was overcome with a remorse which came across to the audience, and we were all briefly moved. A similar tradition to Toone was played in the cellar theatres of Antwerp in the nineteenth century.

In the north of Europe, in Stockholm, there is always something original and exciting going on under the direction of Michael Meschke. A list of the productions by his Marionetteatern over the last twenty years covers an enormously wide spectrum of subjects, each of them done in a different style, all of them original and many of them unique. *King Ubu* was given with a mix of one man (Ubu), small glove puppets and huge flat or built-up cut-outs, all in black and white; *The Little Prince* was done with rod puppets; *Winnie the Pooh* with stuffed animals, slightly shabby as if much loved and used; *Antigone* with black figures as from a Greek vase, handled by the puppeteers all in white – a reversal of accepted practice. *Ferdinand the Bull* was given with shadows, *Woyzek* in masks. Altogether more than sixty productions – we are just scratching the surface. As Meschke and his company have toured throughout almost the whole world, probably being seen in more countries than any

Polish rod and glove puppets from Lodz

other puppet company, it is amazing that he has found time to instigate, let alone bring to completion, such a remarkable body of work.

He is also one of the few puppeteers of this century to enter the political arena. In Britain certainly it is very noticeable how little the Puppet Theatre has had anything to say about either local or world problems, and it would appear that throughout the puppet world nowadays it is rare for any but the most general comment to be made. The Bread and Puppet Theatre of the USA must be excluded from this statement.

In Moscow, in 1976, we saw Meschke's production of *The Splendour and Death of Joaquin Murieta.* This poetic drama Meschke has described as about the brutal murder of a modern South American Robin Hood by the USA because of his incitement of the foreign labour force to revolution. It was performed by actors, each playing many parts, and small figures in little table-top settings. These figures were not articulated in any way but were moved about by the actors. The action when we were there was accompanied by two readers, one Spanish and one Russian.

90

We also had an English interpretation from a Russian girl sitting between us. It is almost impossible to cope with a bombardment of language like this – much better to concentrate on what you can see and let the words wash over you. This we did, and although we obviously missed a great deal the conflict both emotional and physical came through very strongly and a tremendously tense atmosphere was built up. This is of course a type of puppet presentation, even with no language problems, where the acting ability of the humans appears more important than their dexterity as manipulators. But in reality this should not be so, for to be a good operator of puppets one must have acting ability oneself.

This production of Meschke's, culminating in the burning of the USA flag, caused a furore amongst the American delegation in the audience, who took great exception to the light in which their country had been portrayed and regarded it as an insult that it should have been shown in their presence. Meschke countered this with the claim that it was important to show the Russians that in the West we have freedom to comment on the actions of peoples and governments – friend and foe alike. When the Americans appealed to us for our opinion we felt bound to say that no country can set up to be a world power and resent their actions being the object of criticism. The puppet can, and should, be a powerful medium for political comment. This is particularly true of plays which look back to the recent past for their subjects. It is not easy to make instant comment with puppets, the time-lag caused by the need to make the figures is too long.

Tunnel Theatre of Armand Deschamps in Antwerp c1910

Two figures for *Antigone* by Sophocles presented by the Marionetteatern in Stockholm (*photo: Beata Bergstrom*)

Michael Meschke has many plans for the future, including a version of his own of *Don Quixote* and an Irish legend by Yeats. He is particularly interested he says in the idea of mixing all the different arts, not only the dramatic, in what he describes as a 'trans-art-concept'. The results are sure to be exciting and controversial.

In 1952 we were invited to take our Marionette Theatre to Australia. We stayed there for several months and had a most successful tour, playing in New South Wales, Victoria and Canberra. At that time puppets were absolutely unknown in most places in that vast country, in which transport was still very slow and difficult and the country areas very dependent on their own resources for entertainment. There was no television of course and very little cinema in the outback, so that we definitely filled a need and used to play to enormous audiences day after day. At one country town, Ararat, we finished a show to a packed house and were immediately asked by the organisers if we would please do it all over again as there was a huge and eager crowd waiting hopefully outside. We hadn't the heart to refuse – everyone in Australia was always so kind to us – and hurriedly reset and started up the overture.

Travelling a show is always exhausting and with marionettes even more than most, as there is so much equipment to move about and we were only three people to do it, unlike in a repertory company of hefty actors. After our second show in Ararat we were therefore pretty tired and not looking forward to carrying the gear from the hall and loading it in the truck. Suddenly everyone's idea of the ideal Aussie appeared on the stage and asked if he could give us a hand. His name was Peter Scriven; he was tall, handsome and strong, and we learnt later had come into some money which was burning holes in his pockets. He made marvellously light work of the carrying and loading as he told us of his plans to found his own Australian Marionette Theatre. Four years later he presented a large and lavish show called The Tintookies in the Elizabethan Theatre, Sydney. Although Peter has long ago left it for new pastures, the Peter Scriven Company in 1965 became The Marionette Theatre of Australia and is now very much a part of the theatrical scene in that country. It has its own theatre complex and also plays in the famous Sydney Opera House. For the past few years it has been guided by Richard Bradshaw who has directed some very lively and

Chamberlain and Stalin – Nazi propaganda puppets from the collection of Gerald Morice (*photo: Mumford, Kidderminster*)

Poster for The Tintookies from Australia

original programmes. In fact the Australian Puppet Theatre has come a very long way since Peter Scriven talked to us of his plans in Ararat, where we like to think we were in at its conception. And incidentally the word 'Tintookies' is synonymous with 'puppets' in Australia, and the word most likely to be used.

On several occasions when travelling to Australia by those wonderful mail boats which no longer exist, we called in at Colombo in Sri Lanka (then known as Ceylon) and we always went off to look for the local puppets, usually with no success at all. But on one such occasion we were told that a retired judge in the town of Ambalangoda was trying to revive the ancient traditions, and to interest the local young in giving puppet performances. Ambalangoda was apparently a centre not only for puppetry but for all sorts of crafts, such as the highly coloured masks associated with Ceylon. So we hired a taxi and set off through the wonderful lush countryside to see what was going on. We found the judge, Mr Fernando, with no trouble. He was working away in a hall with a pleasant garden surrounding it and quite a crowd of people with him. There were two sad-eyed men who, we were told, were the local traditional puppeteers. They were a Mr G. Lawneris and a Mr G. Jayneris, and for the duration of our brief acquaintance we called them the Gee Brothers. They had with them some of their large and rather fine marionettes which they worked by strings fixed to two rods, in the same way as was done by the old English puppeteers. They were very skilled with these puppets and could make some dance with the correct traditional Eastern movements of the arms, neck and head, and others perform very effective acrobatic tricks. The puppets were about 90cm (3ft) high, with heads modelled from papier-mâché, very well painted and finished and nicely dressed. Two young boys, aged between ten and twelve, were being taught by the Gee Brothers to operate them. They held identical dancing puppets and were practising the same movements over and over again, at the same time stamping their own feet rhythmically so as to ring small bells tied round their ankles. This is a common and very effective accompaniment to Indian and Sri Lankan puppet shows.

Meanwhile, Mr Fernando and some local teenagers were working on a play about a folk character – Mr Mahadenamutta (Mr Know-all) – who was known for the gaffes and mistakes and general chaos he always caused as he went about giving advice and organising things. This was an attempt to resurrect and revive interest in stories which had been popular in the past, an idea we ourselves had tried in Ghana and found unsuccessful. Young people generally do not want to look backward, but to live in the present and look forward. Only after some experience of life does the past appear attractive. But these youngsters were certainly working hard. They had come to a point in the story where a goat had got its head stuck in a jar and, according to Mr Know-All must be beheaded to free it. This required more puppet skill than they possessed and we were happy to show them how to make the head detachable from the body, in a realistic manner. We didn't stay to see what had to happen next!

The Gee Brothers seemed a little aloof from these goings-on and we found it rather difficult to communicate with them. We gathered they were the last troupe still performing in the country, and we were delighted when they agreed to sell us a large and handsome historical puppet character. They told us her name was Ehelopola, and that she had been the wife of a nobleman who had turned traitor to the last King of Kandy and been sentenced with all his family to drowning in Kandy Lake. We have exhibited this puppet in many museums and art galleries in Britain and she is always much admired. After one such exhibition near Bradford she was found to be wearing an extra small silver bracelet round one wrist, presumably a gift from a countryman also far from home.

Ehelopola – marionette from Ceylon (*The Hogarth Collection*)

In India, more than anywhere else, puppet shows are found in their original forms, mostly unaffected until recently by outside influences. The plays they give are based on the stories and characters of the area, whether they are the Mogul legends of the north or the Hindu ones of the south. The personages the puppets represent are indigenous gods, villains or heroes known to all the local people. In Rajasthan, in the north, the puppet shows have never ceased to perform and can still be found moving round the countryside from village to village as they have done for generations, appearing at feasts and fairs and religious and secular occasions throughout the year. The Rajasthani puppets are most attractive, marvellously dressed with stylised but expressive faces. We have three of them in our collection. One is a reversible figure. One way up it is a man, but with a flick of the string (it only has one going from the top to the toe) it reverses and becomes a woman – an invaluable marionette trick. A second character is a Pan-like creature with small horns and cloven hooves, playing a pipe. He is not dressed but painted red and white. No one has ever been able to tell us his name or what part he can have played. But our third character is quite a straightforward one; he is large and good-humoured looking, and smokes a pipe with the assistance of his operator and a rubber tube.

Jan saw one of these wandering troupes in the little town of Brinda-ban, about 200 miles south of Delhi. It was at night by the light of a kerosene lamp, which lit the faces of the audience as much as the pup-pets. The stage consisted of two up-ended beds. A shabby red cloth had been stretched from one to the other to form a proscenium and the backcloth consisted of an even shabbier piece of white material stretched on a rod which had been poked through the rush mattresses about half way up: no drop curtain, no wings and the only entrance for the puppets was to drop them in in full view at the side of the stage. At one side squatted a woman, swathed in sackcloth which also concealed a baby. She beat a tom-tom and chanted a sort of wailing narration to the action, occasionally speaking to the puppets, who replied through their one manipulator, her husband, with the help of a fluttery 'swazzle' sound.

The action took place in the court of King Akbar, the Great Mogul, who was receiving a visit from King Awarsingh and his Cabinet. About a dozen characters, who varied in height from 38 to 50 cm (15 to 20in) apparently according to their importance, came in one by one with much ceremony and bowing, several of them doing clever little dances – even Akbar gave an introductory dance before he, and each of the others in turn, got hitched up with a little jump against the backcloth. They were each controlled by a single loop of string from the top of the head to the small of the back. They had finely carved faces and good costumes. Finally the great dancer, the reason for the assembly, entered. She had four strings, and achieved a surprisingly good Indian dance with them; most Westerners would have needed many more strings to get the same effect.

The rest of the show consisted of various divertisements with variety acts and animals. There was some consternation when the kerosene lamp went out and a puppet camel got caught up with a small oil lamp which had been brought to replace it, and careered round the stage with it dangling from its neck. But no disaster occurred; and perhaps it was meant to happen.

India provides us with yet another legend giving the origin of puppets to set beside those of the Chinese emperor and the Turkish sultan. To our minds it is the most charming of the three, and it attributes the making of the first puppet to Parvati, the wife of Shiva. Having made a marvellous doll she became afraid it possessed evil powers, so she carried it up a mountain and hid it. Shiva, however, followed her, found the doll and was delighted with it. He therefore gave it the power of movement and sent it down to earth to entertain men.

5
SOME UNIQUE AND UNUSUAL PUPPETS

'The perfect puppet resembles us all.'

Gordon Craig

The Sicilian Marionette Theatre

One of the most romantic and dramatic of all Puppet Theatre traditions is that of the Sicilian Marionettes, nowadays alas inevitably reduced to a shadow of what it was in its great days at the beginning of this century. To see a performance today, sitting with a polite audience of cognoscenti in Stockholm or London, or even to see it in Palermo itself amongst the tourists, gives little idea of the experiences chronicled by Festing Jones (*Diversions in Sicily*) in 1911, D. H. Lawrence (*Sea and Sardinia*) in 1924 or Francis Guercio (*Sicily*) in 1938. Except for the reverent productions of religious plays at Easter and Christmas, the sagas performed are always those of Charlemagne and his paladins, wearing heavy armour, in conflict and battle with the Saracens. The audiences of local men used to be violently partisan, and the legends they watched night after night as the story progressed were a part of their own lives and personal history. They knew the terribly complicated relationships between Charlemagne, his knights, and the few women who appear in these stories as if they were members of their own families. They could recognise each knight by the crest on his helmet and would call out their magnificent names as they assembled to do battle or be addressed by their monarch. It is said that the local cabbies named their horses Baiardo and Brighiardoro after the steeds of Rinaldo and Orlando, their great heroes. Barbers also called their razors after the swords of the paladins.

These knights and their opposing Saracens vary in height from 76cm (2ft 6in) to almost life-size. They are worked by two iron rods to the head and hand, with the addition of one or two strings to enable them to draw their swords etc. They can also lower and raise their visors. They don't have strings to their legs but walk with a marvellous jaunty swing from the hips, achieved by twisting the thick wooden knob with which the head-rod is capped, at the same time moving the figure forward. To operate the largest figures the men need to be raised up above stage level, but for the smaller ones they can stand behind wing pieces (there are usually four down each side of the stage) and from there can reach the whole acting area. The story is told by one man, Lui che parla, while crowd noises are provided by the operators and any friends who happen to be backstage, all stamping and shouting as required. There is usually a barrel-organ type of music as well. The legends are told piecemeal, an excerpt every evening until the tale is completed, the whole lasting perhaps nine months or 'two winters' as there were no performances in summer before the days of the tourist trade. The whole audience knew the progress of the saga, and when the evening's extract was known to be tragic, especially the dreadful moment of Orlando's death, the people would be so loathe and therefore so slow getting to the theatre that the performance would be very late in starting, and some people felt unable to go and witness it at all. On the nights when great battles took place, the audience became violently excited and threw objects and abuse at the stage as the great armoured knights were hurled one against the other, swords clashing, blood flowing, limbs and even heads being severed in the fray. Even today these battles can go on for a considerable time until there are literally piles of bodies on the stage. There appears to be a tradition that, if a knight falls, but his rods remain in the operator's hands, he is only wounded and can presently rise up and rejoin the conflict. But if his rods are dropped to the ground, he is a dead man. When a leading personage dies, at the moment of death a small white bird-like apparition flutters upward from the mouth of the character, carrying his soul up to heaven.

We have three of these fascinating puppets in our collection, and although we acquired them at different times they are characters that have a great deal to do with each other in the plays. They are Angelica, Orlando and Astolfo. Orlando falls madly in love with Angelica and, when she spurns him, loses his wits and rushes wildly through the forest. Astolfo, who is known as the English knight, goes off in search of the lost wits, finds them on the moon and returns with them to save Orlando's reason. Although the plots of the plays are those told in Ariosto's *Orlando Furioso*, they are improvised afresh by the speaker every evening and can vary very much according to individual ideas.

There are only three or four women in the whole of these sagas, and although they are often very grandly dressed and bejewelled, the puppet makers do not bother to carve special female bodies for them, but fix their heads on to the same torsos and limbs as they make for the knights, so that our Angelica, with her delicate features and appealing moving eyes, has a most sturdy and masculine pair of legs under her velvet gown. Her arms and hands too could be described as brawny. The very heavy and ornate armour worn by the paladins is said to have been made from melted-down cannon balls left behind by Napoleon's soldiery.

It is interesting to find in two other places – Liège in Belgium and Aachen in Germany – marionette theatres very similar to the Sicilian. In both these cities the same cycles of legends are performed with the same characters and the opposing forces of Charlemagne and the Sara-cens, the large heavy knights in armour, the duels and the battles. In both cities also the puppets are operated in the same manner and staged similarly, although in neither place has the local population identified so strongly with the puppets as in Sicily. On two occasions we saw per-formances by François Pinet and his Marionettes Liègoises, which have been in existence since 1825. The first time the audience consisted of local citizens who obviously knew and enjoyed every moment of the

Puppet from the company of Pinet, Liège, Belgium

show, relishing the fighting and the pageantry, laughing at the humorous exchanges and bawdy jokes, so much so that, although we didn't understand the patois in which it was played, the excitement of the audience was catching and we thoroughly enjoyed the performance. The second time we saw the show it was given before an audience of international puppet players, and although all were appreciative of the skill and dexterity of the performance it never really came to life. It became in fact only academically interesting – a museum piece. We have never managed to see a performance in Aachen where Charlemagne was buried; although we have tried on several occasions we have been unlucky. It is fascinating that such a similar puppet tradition should have grown up in three different countries speaking three different languages. The explanation must surely lie in a folk memory that has passed down through all the generations the dramatic effect felt by the population along the route of the terrible wars of the eighth century.

The Bunraku Theatre of Japan

The Bunraku Puppet Theatre of Japan is undoubtedly the most sophisticated and remarkable puppet theatre in the world today, or possibly at any time. It is at once the most real and the most unreal. Its prestige abroad is enormous, but in its own country it has a constant struggle to survive. Yet in no other land has the greatest of its playwrights written almost entirely for the Puppet Theatre, and in no other country do the live actors go to the Puppet Theatre to study their art. Chikamatsu, who lived from 1653 to 1724, is regarded by many as the equal of Shakespeare, a great playwright and a great poet. He wrote plays for the live Kabuki actors and for the Bunraku, and many of these plays have become interchangeable, being played by both theatres. But the Puppet Theatre has always been regarded in Japan as the purest source of dramatic techniques, and the Kabuki actors still attend the puppet plays as part of their artistic education.

There are three elements in the Bunraku performance, all of them vital. They are the Narrator or Reciter, the manipulators of the puppets, and the musician who accompanies the words and the action on the samisen. The Reciter is the most important in Japanese eyes and his role is so exhausting and arduous that each of the three acts of a play is given by a different performer. The musician and the manipulator are of equal importance. All must go through a long and rigorous training probably starting about the age of ten, and will not be taking part in per-

102

Two scenes from Bunraku plays; (above) *The Love Suicides at Ten-No-Amijima* – note the black hoods of the assistants; (below) the final scene in the play *The Express Messenger to Hades*

formances before an audience until they are in their twenties. The puppet manipulators will be middle-aged before they can undertake the important roles. There are endless conventions that must be remembered. 'A puppet steps forward when asking a question, backwards when refusing a request'; 'a woman steps forward with her right foot, a man with his left foot'; 'a good puppet master does not move his puppet if there is no reason to do so.' The enthusiast who wants to know more should read *The Puppet Theatre of Japan* by A. C. Scott.

Bunraku puppets are about half life-size and often have moving eyebrows and mouths, as well as fingers that can open and close. The manipulators are visible to the audience the whole time as they carry their puppets about on the stage. A principal character will have three manipulators. The chief, who is raised up on high wooden clogs so that his assistants can move around him and under his arms easily, holds the puppet in his left hand and with his right hand works the right hand of the puppet. One assistant works the left hand and the other the puppet's feet. The chief wears the ceremonial samurai kimono and the assistants

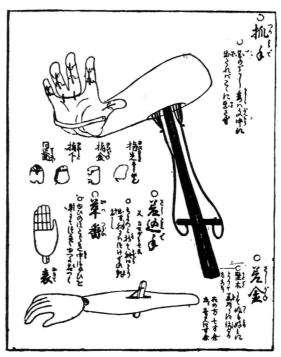

Hand movement of Bunraku puppet (*Gordon Craig's Chapbook No 20 – February 1921*)

are dressed in black, even their hands and faces being covered. It is surprising how soon one ceases to notice the manipulators as they make the puppets perform all the actions necessary for the play. These large dolls develop a quite remarkable life of their own. This is even more astonishing when one realises that, although lesser characters only have one manipulator each, if there are five puppets on the stage there will probably be eleven large humans around operating them!

One of Chikamatsu's plays for the Bunraku, *The Double Suicide* which was based on the actual case of two lovers, is said to have caused such a spate of double suicides that the government of the day banned the writing of any further play on the subject. This particular play is also very interesting because, when it was staged in 1703, the manipulators themselves appeared for the first time holding their puppets in view of the audience. Before that they had always been hidden behind curtains. But it was another thirty years before they started to use three manipulators for each principal character.

We have seen the Bunraku perform several times and it is astonishing how riveting this extremely artificial form of theatre becomes. There are those who maintain that the plays, the style of the puppets, and the method of presentation are all too archaic, perpetuating as they do the ideas and habits of old Japan. But they could hardly be altered without Bunraku being destroyed completely in the process. And in fact we have to bear witness that when the girl in *The Double Suicide* finally winds herself up in her blue sash which draws her inevitably onto her lover's knife and he then kills himself as well, we were extremely moved, as were many members of the 1,500 Australians in the theatre in Sydney where we last saw it.

The Water Puppets of Vietnam

We have long known of these puppets and the image of them has always fascinated us. They are said to have been performing for a thousand years, and yet very few people outside Vietnam have ever seen them. According to the French *Maison des Cultures du Monde* (which has just published a book on the subject), several troupes are still in existence and the marionettes can still be seen in spite of all the country has been through.

The showmen build quite extensive pavilions on landing stages in the lakes with which the country abounds. The sides and back of these pavilions are masked with screens of plaited reeds, through which the

Vietnamese Water Puppet –
Teu the Compere (*photo:
Deutscher, Berlin*)

manipulators can see, but behind which they are invisible to the audience. They move the puppets about on the surface of the water with long underwater rods, up to 9m (30ft) long, each ending in a platform to which the puppet is fixed, and equipped with strings, wires, springs and other devices. The figures, their boats and other properties can be assembled in the concealment of the landing stage, and there the manipulators can rest between performances. When operating the puppets they stand up to their waists in water!

There is an orchestra of drums, gongs and flutes at the side of the pavilion and it plays an important role in the spectacle. The puppets are from 45 to 60cm (18 to 24in) high and give an impression of solidity and smiling benevolence. They are brightly painted in clear colours with a great deal of red and gold. The chief character, a type of Master of Ceremonies, is known as Teu, and is a smiling personage, naked except for a red loin cloth or pair of shorts. There is a great variety of figures, some of them surprising to find on water. There are dancing girls, musicians,

106

fishermen in boats, men waving flags, men with buffaloes and farm implements, even men on horseback and, of course, fish and ducks. There are four fabulous creatures – the Dragon, the Unicorn, The Phoenix and the Tortoise – which take part in all plays, leaping and swimming, flying, dancing and fighting, both on and below the water. The methods of working all these wonders are a closely guarded secret.

Burmese Puppets

The Burmese marionettes are exquisite, beautifully made, dressed and articulated and manipulated remarkably. They vary from delicate little dolls 30 or 38cm (12 or 15in) high to large figures of between 60 and 90cm (2 and 3ft). Animals feature in all the plays and performances, and there is a great deal of dancing. Even the animals all dance. These puppets portrayed a very courtly way of life with much ceremony, and as in Japan the actors of the live theatre would go to the puppets to study movement and gesture.

We have a small collection of these puppets – five Clowns of different sizes, a Tiger, a Red Horse, a Prince and a Princess. They were brought from Rangoon in the early part of this century. When we met the Burmese Cultural Attaché after one of our performances in London several years ago, we asked him if he could tell us about them. He said that the heyday for puppets in Burma was the late-nineteenth century. At that time it was forbidden for any form of love scene to be shown on the stage, but the ban did not apply to wooden actors and the populace consequently flocked to the puppets in large numbers – to the joy of the showmen. But in this century they went into a decline and were at one time almost extinct, although we hear now they are once more on the increase.

The Burmese don't use any form of cross or perch to work their puppets. They hang the loops of string (which in important puppets can be a very large number, some say as many as sixty) over their wrists, and with their fingers grasp and pull the individual strings as they need them. According to Carl Hagermann, a distinguished German writer on puppets, the puppet dancers are made to dance just like the living girls, only more wildly. The girls on the other hand dance as though they are being pulled by strings. The basic movements for both are the same and extremely complicated. A skilled manipulator can produce both realistic and grotesque movements.

The puppeteer's hands are not hidden from the audience, who can therefore watch the precise and skilful movements each hand – and even each finger – makes as it directs the puppets to the music. The movements of the hands are in fact considered equally important to the performance as the puppets which respond to them down below.

Les Veuves

A rare and remarkable use of puppets was seen in the production by Jacques Voyet of *The Widows* by François Billetdoux. The play is about a small French community which is completely dominated by the widows of all the men, who have mysteriously died or disappeared. Only one small boy – an orphan who has appeared from no one knows where – is left, and he is ill. The widows, who are terrified the community will become extinct, are represented by huge rod puppets (called 'shaman puppets' by Voyet) with enormous appealing eyes. Each puppet is carried by a manipulator who is part of the crowd gathered in the market place. At any moment of trouble or crisis these women appear, more than twenty of them, an impressive and terrifying sight rearing up and towering above the distracted humans below. A great deal of the play was obscure to us, but the dramatic effect of the puppets was unforgettable.

Master Peter's Puppet Show

We have had the good fortune to take part in this opera by Manuel de Falla on three occasions, and each one has been an exciting experience.

The first time was on television from the old Alexandra Palace Studios in 1938. Many people don't realise that in Britain at that time we had the only public TV service in the world, transmitting ambitious and adventurous productions every day of the week, and each one a 'first time'! As soon as we knew of the engagement to do *Master Peter* we dropped everything else and started work on it. There was a large number of puppets to be made and a great many problems to be sorted out. The story of the opera is that told by Cervantes of Don Quixote watching a puppet show in the courtyard of an inn. As he watches Charlemagne and his knights playing chess and being called by the heralds to do battle with the Moors, he becomes more and more involved in the play, and when Melisendra (Charlemagne's daughter) and her lover Gayferos are finally captured by the Saracens he is so enraged that he leaps up and, drawing his sword, starts to slash at the puppets, cutting

108

Charlemagne from *Master Peter's Puppet Show* – made by Jack Whitehead for The Hogarth Puppets production for Opera at Ingestre

strings, knocking off heads and bringing the show to an end. The audience is left looking at the showman, Master Peter, grieving over his battered and broken puppets as Don Quixote sings a tremendous aria on chivalry.

We had to make all the figures – eight or nine principals and crowds of Moorish warriors and guards, heralds, horses etc. In addition there were costumes and properties to design, scenic effects to be worked out and the controls and stringing of the marionettes which we would have to learn how to handle. Don Quixote, Master Peter and his Boy were played by live singers. About three weeks before the date of the transmission we started rehearsals for this thirty-minute opera. It was not at that date available on records, so the BBC provided a pianist to play for us to rehearse to. We worked all day and every day for the three weeks, learning the music, planning the moves and getting everything ready to go before the cameras, as we knew we should not have time for much rehearsal in the studio on the day of transmission.

We arrived in good time on that day and set everything up; the orchestra assembled with its conductor Hyam Greenbaum and we met the three singers – Parry Jones as Master Peter, Frederick Sharpe as Don Quixote and Jane Connard as the Boy. Then the conductor took up his baton and we were off. But, horror of horrors, when the orchestra started to play we couldn't recognise one note of what we heard. We are none of us trained musicians and to our ears de Falla's dramatic, difficult and unusual music bore no resemblance to what we had been learning so assiduously on the piano! It was one of the worst moments of our lives. Luckily we kept our heads, and luckily also we had worked so hard that we knew by heart the timing of our movements to each musical passage, so that with the help of occasionally recognising a phrase here and there we managed to struggle through the first rehearsal without disaster. When we had done it two or three times more we felt better and even began to enjoy it, but we shouldn't like to go through that again. It is marvellous music and to work with a real live orchestra and talented singers is a rare treat for puppet players. But when we think of it we always remember the extraordinary and unrecognisable sounds we heard and how we looked at one another and said, 'What's become of the music we've been rehearsing to?'

Twenty years later when we were asked to perform *Master Peter* again there was no problem in securing records to rehearse to. In 1957 we took part in a performance of it at Ingestre Hall, Lord Shrewsbury's stately home in Staffordshire, where he was hoping to establish a permanent home for opera – a Glyndebourne for the Midlands. For us this production was even more exciting than the first, for we would be working with a producer, Anthony Besch, a designer, Peter Rice, and there would be a live audience to play to instead of just the silent television cameras. The singers this time were Alexander Young as Master Peter, Bernard Sonnerstedt as Don Quixote, and Adele Leigh as the Boy. The orchestra was the Royal Liverpool Philharmonic conducted by John Pritchard. In the first part of the evening Purcell's *Dido and Aeneas* was given and then the audience departed to a marquee for a long and leisurely champagne supper during the interval whilst our stage was set up for the second half of the evening. All went excellently, with the audience in a constant ripple of laughter and spontaneous applause breaking out as Gayferos on his gallant steed came galloping to meet his love. We had three sizes of horse and rider to make their way down the mountainside, each getting larger as it drew nearer, until the full-sized pair emerged at ground level. One of the hazards for the puppeteers in this opera is that the Boy will sing for several minutes describing what is about to happen. There is then an indescribable whirl of music lasting a very short time, during which the puppets have to perform intricate and important actions, vital to the plot, and our hearts were in our mouths until they had been accomplished.

We enjoyed very much working with a theatrical producer on *Master Peter*. Anthony Besch, rightly, made no allowances for the fact that he was dealing with puppets and not people and this greatly extended our range and tested our ingenuity. If he asked for a particular move from a figure we had to go away and work at it, all night if necessary, till we could achieve what he wanted. If we had been producing it ourselves we might have settled for an alternative move more easily obtained. We enjoyed working with Alexander Young too. He took his role as Master Peter seriously from our point of view, and would pop round the proscenium to lower the curtain or place a prop in place.

For the period of this production we lived in a caravan in the beautiful park at Ingestre. The weather was lovely; we took our meals in the sunshine in the company of spotted deer and peacocks, and thought that of all ways of earning a living the puppeteer's was the most delightful.

The next year we were asked back to Ingestre to repeat the production of *Master Peter*. The reception was again marvellous, and a few days after it ended Lord Shrewsbury rang us to say he was planning a third season and was hoping to commission Menotti to write a special opera for us. 'Wonderful!' we cried euphorically, 'Why not Picasso to design the puppets?' 'Good idea', said he. Two or three weeks later we heard the earl and countess had decided to part, the house was to be rented or sold and the idea of Opera at Ingestre abandoned.

6
PUPPETS ON TELEVISION

'. . . modern puppets are extraordinary things!'

Gordon Craig

The first involvement the puppets had with television anywhere in the world was in 1930 when Waldo Lanchester, H. W. Whanslaw and Jan Bussell took part in experiments with J. Logie Baird in London. Made up in the peculiar shades for the flickering lights of those days, the puppets went before the cameras in a small studio in Long Acre late at night after the BBC radio station had closed down and Baird had the use of their wavelengths. Apart from variety and circus acts they presented a dramatisation of *The Man with a Flower in his Mouth* by Pirandello. Curiously enough this same play had been put out by Lance Sieveking with live actors from the same studio the night before, thus by a strange fluke scoring two 'firsts' – the first play on TV and the first play with puppets on TV!

When BBC Television opened in 1936 with a public service, puppets were very much in demand. They were small, an advantage both for the cameras and for studio space; they usually came equipped with their own theatres and sets, and their material was already rehearsed and had only to be set in front of a camera. One very early company to appear on the screens was The Jacquard Puppets, a semi-professional group run by John Carr. They became very popular with London audiences for their trio of pianist, violinist and cellist; and for their dramatisation of *No! No! A Thousand Times No!*; *The Moth and the Candle* and other humorous and gentle items all meticulously presented with very small puppets. Picture definition in those early days was nothing like what it is today and many things in the puppet world looked better than they were; but we all had to learn that TV was a great devourer of material – that the visual joke which could be repeated three times in a music hall for instance, and get a bigger laugh each time, could only be done once on

Scene from TV production of *The Man with a Flower in his Mouth* by Pirandello, produced in 1931 in Baird's early studio

television and it was finished. We used to reckon that what lasted three minutes in front of a live audience was over in one minute on television.

We appeared regularly with our own show. Our orchestra quite often introduced the Saturday afternoon programmes, playing in our caravan theatre outside the front entrance of 'Ally Pally'. We also devised and took part in several of what were called 'Communal Shows', when five or six puppet companies would combine to put on a *dance macabre* or an underwater ballet or a Father Christmas extravaganza. We ourselves also made special productions of one-act plays such as Lawrence Housman's *Moonshine*, and *Fly By Night* based on a Boccaccio story. Altogether things were very exciting and the future would have looked very rosy if it hadn't been for the threat of war. Sure enough, television was shut down at the beginning of September 1939 and not until August 1946 did the puppets appear again in the studios of Alexandra Palace.

But when they did get back it was with quite a bang. Not only were the communal shows reintroduced, but on 20 October 1946 Annette Mills and Muffin the Mule appeared and became the nation's favourite personalities. The programmes appeared on Sundays for eight years – I wrote the scripts and manipulated the puppets – until Annette's death in 1954. In fact the BBC claimed that Muffin was the first star to be created by television anywhere in the world. And not only for a children's audience, for in those days everyone watched at tea-time on a

Muffin the Mule with Annette Mills and Ann Hogarth (BBC *copyright*)

Sunday afternoon. People who had TV sets expected to have a tea-party for those in the street who hadn't, and Annette appealed to the Dads as much as Muffin and his friends did to the children.

In those early days, when everything was done live in front of the cameras, we were also all the time working out new methods of presentation and how to use the medium to the best possible advantage, instead of just using it as another form of theatre, reduced and put in a box. One of our early experiments, which is now standard practice, was to use a multiple set. Up to then, settings for puppet plays had been constructed very much as if they were in a theatre or booth, and scenes were changed by lowering a curtain or fading out the camera. But we now did a dramatisation of the *Little Grey Rabbit* stories by Alison Uttley with glove puppets and changed all that. We made a continuous set about 11m (36ft) long, raised up on stilts to a height of about 1·8m (6ft). This set consisted of a landscape in which were included all the venues needed for the thirteen books we dramatised, and in each episode the puppet animals could set out and walk through the long woodland scene until they came to the particular tree, nest, beehive or house called for in the story. With this idea we reckoned we 'liberated the glove puppet from his booth' which had until then contained all his actions.

The *Little Grey Rabbit* series was very popular and we repeated it several times, for new audiences were growing up and television was spreading to other parts of the country. There was only one fly in the ointment and that was the height of the settings. If they were just right for us, they always seemed wrong for the cameramen and gave them terrible backaches. They implored us to put them higher, but then we couldn't hold the puppets up sufficiently high for them to be seen in their proper proportions. They begged us, in that case, to lower them, but then found that our heads appeared in the picture. So we insisted on having it in the optimum position for a good picture and rehearsals were accompanied by the hollow groans of the miserable cameramen. In transmissions they presumably suffered in silence – or at least we never heard them in the stress of our own anxieties.

Many international puppet performers appeared on TV in those years. They were mostly cabaret or music-hall artistes, among them Bob Bromley, René le Strange, Les Marottes, Yves Joly with his Joly Mains, Topo Gigio and many others. But gradually puppets came to be relegated to the children's programmes. Because of the very success of such acts as Sooty, Supercar, Hank, Mr Turnip, Andy Pandy and many others, and because a generation was growing up that had seen so much

Two views of *Little Grey Rabbit* series on television showing part of the wide set and close-up shots of puppets (*BBC copyright*)

puppetry on television in its childhood, the idea got around that puppets were only for children – kid's stuff! It wasn't until recently, with the phenomenal success of *The Muppets* followed by the bitter and always unsympathetic *Spitting Image*, that puppets began to claw their way back precariously into the adult programmes.

We used to appear on television in many different places – in America, Australia and Canada as well as in most European countries. One place we liked going to very much was Luxembourg, where the studio was set in a beautiful park in the middle of the city and where the atmosphere was so relaxed and friendly that families used to wander in from the surrounding grounds and watch what was going on. They were never driven out by the staff and never took advantage of the privilege, but just stood and watched from around the doorways. It was a small studio run by a few extremely able people who did everything that needed doing. Never was a set-up so free of rules and regulations or argument about who did what. Our main problem was with the local language in which the programme went out. On one occasion we were told that as soon as we heard our name 'The Hogarth Puppets' from the studio announcer we were to spring into action. When we finally heard the words 'Oggarts Pippins' it was a second or two before we recognised it.

Every generation probably thinks they 'had the best of it'. Certainly it was marvellous for the TV performer who knew that at the moment he was performing all the viewers were watching because there was no alternative, and because everything was 'live' and because so much of what we did was being done for the first time ever. Certainly there is much more competition now. But there are many more opportunities too. It's still the case of being the right person in the right place at the right time. We also remember the old music-hall artist who was sorry for people like us who could only do something on the telly once and everyone had seen it. 'I could do my act on the halls for fifteen years', he told us, 'polishing it and improving it all the time.' Certainly there must be a lot of material around now that never gets a chance of being polished and improved. But every age has its compensations. The uncertainty of 'live' television has gone now that everything is recorded, and with the latest inventions it is no longer necessary for the strings of the puppets to show, or the hands and faces of the manipulators to intrude into a picture in error! Great advantages! But on the other hand the public is much more jaded and surfeited – nothing is a marvel to them now. They would no longer ask on Monday morning, 'However did you make Muffin do that?'

117

7
TRAVELLING SHOWS
AND STREET THEATRE

'For here comes the fortune telling ape and the puppet show'
Cervantes

Puppet players have always been travellers, usually playing in the open air, going to where their public was, in the villages or towns at times of holiday or festival. It is probable that the first 'puppets' were in fact idols or effigies of saints, carried through the streets at religious ceremonies and made to move their heads or hands by the priests who tended them in order to impress their simple flocks. They were not giving a theatrical performance, but probably inspired others to do so. All through the ages we find descriptions of travelling puppet shows – in China, Japan, India, Greece, Turkey and all across Europe. For the itinerant showman in the seventeenth and eighteenth centuries, a couple of 'dancing dolls' jigging on a board by means of a string attached to his foot and keeping time to his pipe or drum, was easily carried around and set down in the street or market place. One such is portrayed in the foreground of Hogarth's 'Southwark Fair'. There are also several paintings and engravings to be seen of French and Italian performers of this kind, known as *marionettes à la planchette* and much more elegant to look at than the English one. We have had two sets of similar (though even more primitive) 'dancing dolls' sent us within the past few years from different parts of Africa. There the showman sits on the ground with outstretched legs and fixes the little crude wooden figures with thongs between his big toes. Humming and slapping his thighs he makes the puppets jig, and hopefully extracts a few coins from passers-by. When we tried it we found it extremely painful after a very few moments of slapping.

The puppet show described by Cervantes in *Don Quixote* was of a much more elaborate kind than the foregoing, but was probably still carried from inn to inn on its owner's back, as was the Punch and Judy

118

booth described by Dickens in *The Old Curiosity Shop.*

In the nineteenth century, the big marionette shows had to play in halls and theatres. They were too vulnerable to the weather and too elaborate to set up in the open air, but they still travelled enormous distances, moving sometimes daily under conditions of extreme discomfort and even danger. The reader of *The Life and Travels of Richard Barnard Marionette Proprietor,* as recorded in his diaries and issued by the Society of Theatre Research in 1981, finds it hard to credit the appalling hardships and misadventures suffered by this showman and his wife and children as they journeyed around Europe, reaching as far afield as Russia and Romania, travelling in carts and waggons, sometimes pulled by bullocks, with babies being born, children falling ill, managers defaulting and every possible calamity happening to them. It appears that, as in all branches of theatre, the puppet showmen were – as they still are – dedicated to their calling, fascinated in some way by their puppets, and always sure that success and good fortune were just around the corner.

A showman of a very different kind – a man of intellect and education, but one who took to the road and because of his own writings is probably the best known of the travelling puppeteers, was Walter Wilkinson. With his theatre, puppets and possessions he walked the

The first caravan theatre. 1940

roads between the villages of Britain in the 1920s and 1930s and wrote a succession of books such as *The Peepshow, Vagabonds and Puppets, A Sussex Peepshow* etc, giving not only a picture of life in rural Britain at that period but an idea of the philosophy which guided him. Since his day puppets have become motorised and, except for Punch and Judy, play mostly indoors in this country at least.

In 1940 we bought a trailer caravan, secondhand. It was melon shaped and we immediately set about converting it into a theatre. We cut a proscenium-opening in one side and a hole in the roof, and made a lid with canvas sides which could be raised to give us head room when we stood above the stage performing. We gave one or two shows to try it out and then undertook an engagement with the London County Council in their first ever Holidays at Home programme in the London parks. The war was at its height and the children of London were spending their nights and much of their days in the Underground shelters. The idea was to get them up for fresh air and entertainment. We were the LCC's guineapigs. At the first park we arrived at we found 2,000 people waiting for us, and when they saw the small caravan theatre they panicked and mayhem ensued. This story has been told in another book, *Puppet's Progress*, by Jan Bussell.

But the whole experience of these wartime shows was a quite extraordinary one, with the pale, unhealthy looking children, smelling of the shelters, blinking at the sunlight like prisoners from their dungeons and not quite sure what was going to happen. We quickly learned the necessary technique – never to arrive too soon. One had to be ready to start ten minutes or so after arrival as the audience were on a very short fuse, always afraid of missing out on something or not getting the best possible position. We learned too never to hang around after the show was over, but to get away as soon as possible. While we were there the children were restless – was there more to come? The most important lesson was to keep the Mums and Dads and Grandmas well away at the back. Children on their own were always manageable; it was the parents who fought. We gave three performances a day for a period of five or six weeks, each show in a different park. It was a gruelling schedule, which we did annually for twenty-five years. And for most of that time, particularly in the early years, it was very rewarding, for the need for it was so obviously great.

The children's memories were surprisingly long. If we brought on a puppet which had appeared the previous year a great cry of 'Seen it! Seen it!' would go up. To which the puppet would bellow back 'Oh! No,

Handbill for Happenstance

you ain't!' as it went into a perfectly new routine. They also knew their rights. One day a drenching thunderstorm broke over the defenceless children sitting crowded on tarpaulins which were soon awash and soaking. We were all right, snug under our roof, but suggested to them they should all run home and get dry. The reply came back at once 'You go on! You're paid for it, ain't yer?' And they stayed to the bitter end – with no complaints.

We remember also a small urchin who came up to us as we were setting up in a very rough and tough park to which we had only reluctantly agreed to return, the previous year's experience having convinced us we were not really their sort of show – or at any rate they weren't our sort of audience. 'Saw your show last year', he said. 'Oh, yes.' 'There was a cake in it!' 'Yes, there was, that's right.' 'Who ate it?', he then asked with great anxiety. Obviously we had made an impression, if only on his stomach.

But after twenty-five years we felt it was time to stop. There was no longer the same pressing need for these children to be entertained in the parks. They all had a daily intake of amusement. In fact some made it plain they had difficulty fitting us in between their TV schedules. Besides the parks were getting noisier; buses and lorries roared by non-stop, aeroplanes screamed overhead, radios were everywhere and the petrol fumes nearly suffocated us as we took in the deep breaths necessary to make ourselves heard above everything else. So we called it a day, with regret in many ways, for it had been a worthwhile stint, teaching us a lot about human nature in general and ourselves in particular.

Of late years a different kind of open-air entertainment with puppets has appeared, called Street Theatre. In this the audience is no longer passive and stationary, required to be merely spectators. On the contrary they take an active part, helping to carry and manipulate the huge figures, accompanying them through the streets, and in fact very often many of them become involved long before the show, in the actual making of the figures. In some ways it can be likened to a return of the Mystery and Morality plays of medieval times.

At the big puppet festival which takes place every three years in Charleville in France, the whole affair is rounded off with a Street Theatre event, with a large number of young people spending a lot of their time and energy through the festival period planning and making and rehearsing a gigantic spectacle to wend its way into the marvellous old square in the town centre and bring the festivities to a riotous conclusion.

A street theatre production by Happenstance, designed by Tony Lewery, Cheshire (*photo: Ross Williams*)

In the USA, the Bread and Puppet Theatre directed by Peter Schumann holds an annual spectacle in a natural amphitheatre in Vermont. Here enormous crowds of tourists gather and participate in a 'happening' built round a current issue.

Tony Lewery, who since 1977 has run Happenstance Theatre in Cheshire, believes that 'people enjoying themselves are in an ideal mood for rediscovering a few simple but optimistic home truths'. He gives street shows with giant puppets for both children and adults, and celebrates local community events such as Bonfire Night and Hallowe'en.

The Chinese and Indians have always mounted tremendous processions with leaping lions, dragons and mythical creatures. Perhaps Puppet Theatre is here returning to its roots – the priests with their idols. Only nowadays the figures are as likely to be being held up for abuse or recrimination as for veneration, and the theme of the performances is probably political rather than spiritual. But like all entertainment it serves a valuable purpose, releasing pent up feeling, engendering excitement and interest and generally drawing people together to share an experience or an emotion, to see another point of view, or just to enjoy themselves and feel part of a larger whole.

8

BLACK LIGHT, ULTRA VIOLET, CHROMA KEY AND STOP-ACTION

There are still many different kinds of puppet we have not mentioned. In fact there is no established definition of what constitutes a puppet and what does not. There are no rules, one can do as one wishes, wear masks or climb into a costume, hang the figure round one's neck, even put one's own feet into its shoes, operating the body with rods from the elbows – or work under water. After all, it is what the performer has to say that really counts.

In Victorian times they started to experiment with black-light theatre. For this technique dim 'dazzler' lights are shone at the audience, and the narrow area in which the puppets are to appear is brightly lit from the sides. The manipulators, dressed in black velvet, with black hoods and gloves, are able to handle the figures with the help of short horizontal rods from behind, keeping out of the light themselves and so remaining invisible. This technique has been perfected by the Black Theatre of Prague and its offshoots. It is also used in many of the large East European puppet theatres, who cunningly employ brightly lit rod puppets in the front of the stage as 'dazzlers' and fill the back and upper half of the stage with figures worked in black light.

A similar technique is used with ultra-violet light, which causes the appropriately painted puppets to shine out luminously. But the range of colours available is restricted and the effect is really only good for a short variety item, such as a dance with rather gaudy flowers or perhaps a comic *Danse Macabre* with skeletons.

A more serious and successful use was made of this technique by the Marionette Theatre of Australia while we were in charge there, when Charles Dlask produced Benjamin Britten's *Guide to the Orchestra* with all the instruments luminous in this way. His ultra-violet production of Prokofiev's *Peter and the Wolf* was also interesting, although perhaps not quite so successful.

Television has revolutionised the possibility of puppeteers actually handling their puppets – rather like the Japanese Bunraku – but remaining completely invisible. This is the technique of chroma key, by which the camera refuses to record anything of a certain colour. Thus there is no need for performers to sweat it out in black-velvet costumes and hoods. On arrival at the studio one is handed blue body tights with sleeves, gloves and head mask of the same material. In the normal bright studio lights one can see through this quite easily and all one has to be careful about is not letting one's hands or any part of one's body come between the camera and the puppet. Furthermore the figure can be superimposed onto a painted background perhaps only a couple of feet wide, taken on another camera.

Puppets can even be worked by remote control. Electronic mouths and eyes worked off the sound tape were introduced by Gerry Anderson in his *Supercar* and *Thunderbird* films. Soon there will be little need for the puppeteers to go along at all!

There is always controversy about which category stop-action puppets fit into. For example, we certainly count Lotte Reiniger as a puppeteer, because not only did she occasionally give live shows herself, but has designed and cut several different productions for us to perform live. But of course her international fame rests on her pioneer work in the field of stop-action with her silhouette films. Yet the figures she uses for these are identical in construction to those she has made for us. In our case we attached them to rods and operated them against a vertical screen: in her case the figures and scenery were placed on a ground-glass table-top with a light underneath and a camera above. She would move each figure a minute fraction between taking each frame of the film – achieved by pulling a chain hanging from the camera. Although the number of frames needed for a certain sequence, passage of music or sentence of dialogue was mathematically worked out beforehand, Lotte's sensitive fingers had a truly magical and life-giving touch. One of the most striking examples of her skill was in her Nativity play. In this there is an Elephant and a Palfrey. Without the help of mathematics Lotte somehow makes something quite moving in the way the little pony has to trot along to keep pace with the lumbering elephant. Certainly this is puppetry.

There is also Trinka, the famous Czech stop-action artist and innovator, one of whose best-known films was Shakespeare's *Midsummer Night's Dream* – although the cut Anglicised version was pretty drear. Today in Britain we have Cosgrove Hall who made one of the finest stop-action films we have ever seen, of the *Pied Piper*. And there are others too numerous to mention. These artists work with beautifully modelled figures whose secret joints are concealed under layers of rubber and costume. They can even change their facial expression, move their fingers and pick things up. They are worked frame by frame in elaborate model settings. To move them the small amount between each take requires an incredibly steady hand – a clumsy push and perhaps the whole sequence must be started again, taking days or even weeks. One of the greatest difficulties is to make them keep their balance when walking, and for this one or other of the feet has to be firmly fixed on the ground. This is sometimes achieved by numerous holes underneath the covering of the stage floor, through which plugs can be pushed into a foot; or by making the floor of something a bit sticky like Plasticine; or even by using magnets.

Where to draw the line between this and drawn cartoon as a form of puppetry is not quite clear. But when all is said and done we do not believe in separating all these different means of expression into categories. Artists should be free to use any or all mediums to express themselves, and can widen their technique enormously by studying and learning from every aspect of Theatre, Television and Cinema.

9
FANFARE FOR PUPPETS

'He who invented puppet shows was a greater benefactor to his species than he who invented operas'

William Hazlitt

We should like to try to express now something of what we have learned in our life amongst the puppets and how the Puppet Theatre looks to us after fifty years of its pains and pleasures. At times people laugh at us. 'They just play with dollies', an old boy in our village was heard to say, and at times we laugh at ourselves. But at heart we do think very seriously about it all.

Let us start with the puppet itself. Making it must surely be more than an aimless exercise in craftsmanship; there must be some theatrical purpose in its creation. We believe a good puppet, like a good sculpture, should always carry some intrinsic message, its creator's view of what it represents, an exaggeration perhaps, certainly some sort of intensification – an isolation and therefore concentration of particular qualities conveying the artist's impression of his subject. Secondly, it has to move well and have the capacity in its construction and jointing to take the attitudes and make the gestures required of it in the rôle it is to play. Thirdly, the play, sketch, recitation, dance or song it is to perform must be suitable material for puppet interpretation. Obviously puppets are not suitable for realistic drawing-room comedy, or sit-com fare. Furthermore different kinds of puppet would seem more suitable for different kinds of performance: glove puppets for knock-about fun, shadow puppets for poetic fantasy, rods for noble and romantic drama and marionettes for all-round purposes with perhaps the emphasis on dance and mime. But these are only very general rules, proved by many remarkable exceptions.

So what is the real purpose of the Puppet Theatre? What is its raison d'être? Speaking very generally it should not exist to emulate the human

127

theatre, but like the human theatre it must be concerned with people, with society, with the world in which we live. One of the striking things one sees as one looks around the puppet world is its extraordinary variety. The basic material of the human theatre is the actor. But the basic material of the Puppet Theatre is not flesh and blood. Its actors can be specially made for the job. Not only that but, as we have shown, they can be presented in so many different ways, with techniques ranging from those thought of a thousand years ago, tried and tested by time, to those made possible only now by inventions in materials, in lighting, in sound equipment and so on. But all these things must be used not for their own sakes but to convey something, to comment in some way; to involve at different times the sympathy, the horror, the incredulity, in fact the whole range of the emotions of an audience. For the puppet as well as for the player – 'the play's the thing!'

There are a number of stage plays which adapt well for puppets. Two obvious choices are by the Czech author Carel Capek – *R.U.R.* about a robot factory in which the robots take over, and *The Insect Play* in which a Tramp observes and comments on the characteristics of various insects – the warlike ants, the greedy beetles with their precious balls of dung, etc. The field of opera also offers opportunities. We have already mentioned *Master Peter's Puppet Show,* but the best example we know of an opera suitable for puppets is Ravel's *L'Enfant et les Sortileges.* It is in fact an opera which demands to be done by puppets. You have only to look at the list of characters – a Chinese Cup, a Tree, a Tom Cat, a Teapot, a Frog, the Fire, an Animal etc. It is about a bad-tempered small boy who won't do his homework and gets up against everyone and everything. The fire and the ashes come out of the grate and attack him; the figures on the wallpaper – Shepherds and Shepherdesses which he slashes – come to life and remonstrate with him; the mathematical Ciphers in his exercise book, the Armchair, the Clock, the Tree, all defend themselves against him. There is a glorious duet for two Cats. The idea of casting such parts from well-known opera singers seems to us ludicrous. Yet only once have we seen the opera done by puppets – an amateur group at that – and it was brilliantly satisfying.

We have said that puppets are a marvellous medium for satire and comment, but perhaps above all they can excel in fantasy. Plays involving gods, demons, fairies, characters which can defy gravity, or fly, or lose a head and juggle with it, or transform themselves into something quite different (their alter egos or 'auras' perhaps) are quite possible in the puppet theatre. For plays with casts of animals, whether used to satirise the human world or to present the cosy life beloved of children, puppets obviously have an advantage over humans dressed up. A puppeteer we much admire, though he is not often seen, is Feike Boschma of Holland. He opens a suitcase which appears to contain some pieces of wood and limp gauze-type material, and draws out a miraculous, phantom-like, prancing Horse – mane tossing, hooves flying – a wraith of a horse, but one which sums up all the characteristics of the animal. *The Muppets*, on the other hand, endow their animals with very human personalities. We have all known Miss Piggys, Kermits and the rest. Puppets of toys, such as Andy Pandy and Teddy, or Sooty, also act like human children; whereas Rod Hull's Emu behaves like no emu – or human – ever known. It is purely a puppet creation.

We have in our repertoire many puppets not only of inanimate objects such as the Spirits of Gold, Silver and Precious Stones, but representations of elements like Fire, Mist, Rain, Wind and Lightning. For followers of the weather forecasts we also have an Anti-cyclone as-

Gold and Silver, puppets made by Jan Bussell for a ballet, part of a production of *Bluebeard*

sociating with a Deep Depression. Scenes or plays set under water with all the strange, fantastic creatures to be found there, or in a churchyard at midnight with skeletons, ghosts, and spirits of all kinds, are splendid subjects for puppet plays, mimes or ballets. Scenes can be set in toyshops, amongst the inhabitants of a flowerbed with conversations between caterpillars, or between two suitcases complaining of rough treatment by British Rail – the list is endless.

Although the subject matter for plays for the Puppet Theatre is very wide, authors are reluctant to write for it. This is explainable in part because in our modern society there is not a public prepared to go to puppet theatres, which they regard as only for children. This public could be created, it is only lying dormant; but it needs a radical, new approach by all concerned, authors, managements and puppeteers. We must get away from the idea that because puppets are usually small they can only be used for trivial, light, jokey material and never expect to move people or make them think.

We were first made aware of the ability of the Puppet Theatre to present the great emotions, the dramatic events, when we produced *Macbeth* with stylised figures. We were impressed by teenagers who told us that they could enjoy and understand the great speeches and soliloquies when they saw Shakespeare's larger-than-life characters performed by our symbolic figures. They weren't distracted by the human

A sea battle from The Hogarth Puppets production of *Aucassin and Nicolette*

Scene from The Hogarth Puppets production of *Macbeth*, puppets designed and made by Michael and Jane Eve

element. As one girl put it, 'the actors always get between me and what the character is saying'.

In fact here we are getting back to the Mask, where the real actor is concealed by his stylised, artificial face, leaving the audience free to deal only with the emotions he is expressing. The puppet replaces not only the actor's face but the whole of him. It is the complete embodiment of the character. And what then becomes so fascinating is that even a small puppet, if skilfully carved and manipulated, is found capable of expressing the most enormous emotions. The concentration of the audience and the puppeteer upon this animated symbol, starkly conveying its message without any human distractions or contradictions, is amazing.

If authors could only realise all this they would seize upon the great stories of the world, with their joys and sorrows, merciless fates, relentless greed, misery and evil, and write plays about them for actors made to their specifications, and not just for human actors who happen to be available at the moment. We would never hear the phrase, 'Of course there's no one around now who could play . . .'. He could be designed and made to everyone's satisfaction. Is this a joke? No! A dream? Yes!

10

TO BE A PUPPETEER!

We have told of the different kinds of puppet in different parts of the world and tried to convey our own pleasure and excitement about them. Perhaps we may have inspired a few people to attempt some practical study of the art. There are numerous books available on the making of puppets, details of joints, staging, materials etc, but here we offer some broad principles, and sound a few warnings.

Glove Puppets

There are many ways of presenting glove puppets. The simplest, for performing to a small number at home say, or for hospital work, is to use a table-top booth with the proscenium-opening starting about 30cm (12in) up from table level. The manipulator sits with his elbows on the table, and his head and shoulders concealed by a backcloth sufficiently thin for him to be able to see his puppets silhouetted through it when the light is in front. For larger audiences table level is too low, and so one uses a floor-standing booth just a bit higher than the puppeteer when he is standing. But this idea of having one's face behind the backcloth is in fact very restricting, and it is much better to make the booth even higher – as indeed most Punch and Judy men do – and work the puppets at arm's length. In this way wonderful chases can be staged, and puppets are free to turn right round, by means of the showman turning round himself with his back momentarily to the audience. It is however very exhausting working with one's hands above one's head until one's muscles get used to it. In order to get into training we ourselves used to sit in front of the TV in the evening with our hands up for as long as we could endure it, causing a friend coming in unexpectedly to ask anxiously, 'Where's the hold-up?' But we did get so that we could work quite a long show this way without discomfort.

Some of the French Guignol booths have become very elaborate, like miniature theatres, with numerous backcloths, borders and wing

The Old Woman Who Lived in a Shoe – Sally McNally's show for small children

pieces, which can be flown high above the acting area until needed, and with elaborate three-colour lighting systems. This type of show involves using considerable depth of scenery, and the danger arises, if the audience is too low compared with the proscenium height, that when the puppets move away from the front of the stage they begin to sink from sight and get lost. This can be counteracted to some extent by having the seating raked. But of course if the back rows get too high they will begin to see the heads of the manipulators. So the lines of sight have to be worked out very carefully.

Earlier in this book we have described how Therese Keller worked on more than one level in a small booth and how in our rod production of *Europa* we developed this on a large scale (page 61), but of course it is not necessary to have a booth in the accepted sense at all. Sally McNally, playing for very small children, appears in costume as The Old Woman Who Lived in a Shoe, sitting in her booth which is shaped like a shoe, and she can thus talk to the puppets or the audience. She can duck down and work kneeling for any moments when the puppets must be alone for the plot and she doesn't want to be seen. There must be many variants of this sort of idea.

It is more usual to have a screen 1·8 to 2·4m (6 to 8ft) wide and just high enough to hide the operator's head. This can be dressed up to represent the setting for a particular play, say a street, a castle, or a meadow, perhaps with an occasional tree. It helps to have something, such as a house or a rock at the outside edges to provide a wing from which the puppets can make their entrances.

Whatever method of presentation is used, lines of sight must be considered. For example, a low booth is good for playing to children sitting on the floor, but an audience in rows of chairs might have difficulty in seeing. On the other hand children on the floor must be kept well back if a high booth is being used, or they will have to strain upwards, and even so may not see all that is happening. We were once invited to see a glove-puppet show and the booth was so high that we never saw more than the top of a puppet's head, and part of the time saw no puppets at all! One must also be careful not to get the front rows too wide.

It is important to have a good solid 'playboard'. This should only be a few inches wide, and run along the bottom edge of the proscenium or along the top of the screen if no proscenium is being used. It is essential for putting down props, or fixing small bits of scenery, the hangman's noose for example, pieces of furniture, trees etc. Glove puppets love to smack their hands down on it when making a point.

Whatever the material used for making glove-puppet heads they should be very light and the result should be very bold to carry to an audience. The neck is part of the head, not separately jointed, and should have a groove round its base into which the costume can be attached. Hands can be made of wood or felt or washleather, with a short hollow length of arm for attaching to the puppet's sleeve or to an extension tube if one is used. Generally it is a mistake and distracting for an audience to give a figure a moving mouth unless it is a singer or some ape-like character with a huge jaw – or an animal. But it is possible to arrange a hinged lower jaw that can be operated by the tip of the finger inside the puppet's neck; or alternatively to have it controlled by a string running down inside the costume.

It is a good idea to sew large curtain rings onto the back of the puppets' costumes, at the bottom, so that they can hang upside down on a row of hooks inside the front of the booth. In this way you can quickly hang a figure up when it exits and plunge your hand into another – while still keeping a character acting like mad up on stage!

People are inclined to think that the glove puppet is the easiest kind of puppet to manipulate. In fact to be theatrically effective with anything so simple requires considerable histrionic talent. One must practise in front of a mirror for a long period, discovering the different gestures and body attitudes that are possible. One of the things to be avoided is keeping the puppets' hands sticking permanently upwards (the most comfortable position for one's fingers). Glove puppets are particularly good at handling small properties, picking things up, putting them down with a flourish, and even throwing things to each other, all of which requires much practice. Puppets with tube extensions in the sleeves are inclined to be more clumsy at these tricks and will need more rehearsal.

But one mustn't spend too long in front of a mirror. One must become so accustomed to the stretch of one's arms to the correct playing height for the booth as to fall into that position automatically. A great problem is to hold the height during a long scene, and more especially where you have varying heights, for example a trainer with an animal, a teacher with a small boy. The teacher must never accidentally shrink to the boy's height, nor must the boy grow momentarily to be a giant. We once had a very long scene to play in the *Little Grey Rabbit* series with two animals in a boat. It was agonising to keep them sailing calmly around the pond, chatting of this and that – even half an inch too low and they appeared to be sinking unconcernedly into the water.

135

Walking is another thing to study carefully. Everyone has a characteristic walk, some bouncy, some dragging, according to age and mood. With practice one should achieve these effects without having to think of them as one throws oneself into the part. The real mastery comes when you can play two parts on the stage at the same time, keeping their voices and movements differentiated. No: it's not easy!

Rod Puppets

Most of the foregoing remarks on Gloves apply equally to rod puppets. Structurally rods require a wooden shoulder-piece and solid arms, jointed at shoulder, elbow and wrist. They can also have legs. The arm joints can be extremely simple, perhaps just a piece of string or a leather bootlace. But the neck joint is a bit more complicated. Basically a hole is made in the shoulder piece through which the neck is passed, after which a stop, such as a thick ring, must be glued to it to prevent the shoulder-piece sliding off, whilst the neck is free to turn. The neck, which should be able to move quite freely, can be grasped inside the chest of the puppet, or it can be fixed to a rod which carries on down to be manipulated below the puppet, passing inside its skirt or running between the legs. Sometimes it travels inside a leg, making a walking movement possible, but still able to twist and make the head turn. But this technique is only used by the more advanced and professional theatres. Some of these theatres, following the teaching of Obrastzov, have this rod terminate inside the chest as a handle resembling the butt of a revolver, with a trigger to make the head nod, working against a spring in the neck to pull it up again, and a small knob which can be gripped between finger and thumb to turn the head from side to side.

It is customary in these more elaborate productions to have several people manipulate one puppet. The chief manipulator is responsible for the head movement and body attitude, a second manipulator is in charge of the hands, while a third works the legs, with rods to the soles of the feet. Naturally this requires the most detailed planning or choreographing of the puppet's movements and great discipline from the manipulators, whose own movements must be rehearsed with equal exactness. The effect obtained thus can be astonishingly realistic. In a simplified version the revolver-like handle to the head rod would come inside the chest of the puppet, there would be no legs, and the one manipulator would also manage the arms, working both hand-rods in his free hand, sometimes letting one of them drop to concentrate on some special gesture with the other. Some people believe that the individual freedom this gives a solo performer makes for a more spontaneous and lively interpretation of the puppet character portrayed.

A brief hint may be helpful about the fixing of the arm rods on the puppet's hand. The rod should terminate as a stiff wire (in the case of a small puppet it could consist entirely of wire with just a short wooden handle). The end of the wire should be bent into a small loop, inserted into a groove in the puppet's hand or wrist, and held in position by a pin or small nail; the groove must be cut sufficiently long to allow the wire considerable play backwards and forwards. With this joint a truly amazing control is possible, allowing the arm to take up almost any position and gesture most realistically.

Shadow Puppets

There are several distinct ways of operating shadow puppets. The very large Indian shadow puppets, often almost life size and made from the skins of various animals treated to transparency, are held by the manipulators standing immediately behind them, clutching short wooden handles to the head and arm but keeping far enough back so as not to interfere with the row of lights between themselves and the screen. These lights are usually arranged like a theatrical batten above their heads, and are sometimes replaced these days with long electric strip-lamps. Of course originally they were oil lamps.

The Javanese figures, however, are very much smaller, averaging about 60cm (2ft) tall, and are operated from below the screen with vertical rods. The single light is placed 1·8 or 2·4m (6 or 8ft) back, shining over the top of the squatting Dalang's head. Being so far back produces a very clear, hard shadow on the screen, whereas the nearness of the Indian lights gives a much more blurred image. However, with these large figures a little blurring is not important and may even add a certain mystique.

The Chinese also use a light well back from the screen. The manipulators stand to work the puppets and the light plays over their heads, high enough not to cast their shadows on the screen. The puppets from Peking are surprisingly small – about 30cm (12in) high, those from Setschuan about 60cm (2ft). The Chinese have developed a unique style using donkey skin treated to render it very thin and transparent. The colours of course shine through the screen in the same way as the light shines through a stained-glass window, and the costumes are painted in bright reds, golds and blues, with transparent vegetable dyes. This, with the elaborate stencilling and the delicate cutting – the profile of a face for instance is cut out scarcely thicker than a hair – produces the most exquisite effect on the screen. The various joints are made by fastening two pieces together with a stitch of cotton, and the figures mostly have three wires to control them: one to the neck and one to each hand. These wires are stitched on quite loosely, so that they can fold flat for packing, but are held more or less horizontally for operating, or they can be placed at an angle resting on the floor behind the screen, holding the puppet in place against it.

The oldest Turkish and Greek shadow puppets are made from camel skin, but these days one often finds them made from coloured plastic which of course allows the colours to shine brightly through the screen. They vary in height from about 30cm (12in) for the Turkish to 60 to 90cm (2 or 3ft) for the Greek, and the joints are often made by means of loose rivets. The skin and other material used is quite thick and stiff, un-like the heavily scraped and treated Indian and Chinese figures which, though in fact surprisingly tough, give an impression of being very fragile. The Turkish and Greek tradition, very much younger than the others, has one great manipulative advantage in that the rods are firmly fixed horizontally to the puppets. This gives an extra twisting facility, for example to wag a finger with the rod fixed to a pointing hand, or nod a head with a rod fixed to the top of the head using a neck joint – or even a double joint, one at each end of the neck. But the standard Turkish style is to use only two rods, one for one hand (the other arm being cut in a fixed position) and the other rod at the shoulder. Normally there is no neck joint. These rods are about 60cm (2ft) long and a row of lights is placed underneath them, rather like footlights but behind the screen. All Turkish and Greek figures, and also the Chinese, are cut in profile.

Modern exponents of Shadow Theatre in the West no longer use skin, but plastics for coloured figures, and card or metal for black and white effects. Most of Lotte Reiniger's marvellous figures were made in card, with occasional bits of lead for weighting. Sometimes a dash of colour is added by sticking a small piece of plastic (the kind of material that is used for coloured lighting in the theatre) with Sellotape over an incision, say a belt or a scarf. When making a fully coloured puppet great care must be taken where parts overlap at a joint, producing a third colour on the screen. Sometimes this effect can be made use of, but one way of avoiding it is to incorporate a black, non-transparent shadow to cover the joint. A quick way of making joints is to use the split-pin type

Fig 1 Fixing rods for shadow puppets

of paper clip, making large enough holes and not pressing the ends too tightly so that the parts move freely.

A very useful way to fix the rods which incorporate the Turkish possibilities of horizontal manipulation with the Chinese ability to prop the figures against the screen or fold them flat with their rods when packing, was invented by the Australian shadow player Richard Bradshaw (Fig 1). The idea is to hinge the rod to the puppet by bending the end of the wire at right angles and Evo-stiking it down to the figures with a small square of cardboard. If the end of the wire has its tip bent at a further right angle this will stop it pulling out of the hinge. Many German puppeteers prefer to work their figures from below using clear Perspex in place of rods or wires, and sometimes a thread running through eyes fixed to the puppets to obtain additional movements.

An ordinary light bulb hanging more or less in front of one's face (screened from the eyes with a shade) as one is manipulating provides a very good and convenient light source. Of course the puppet's rods will also create shadows. But if a strip lamp is used this is largely obviated. We sometimes use colour-wheels behind the screen for special effects, and shining different colours through coloured puppets or objects can produce very interesting results. Television and film people usually make a great fuss about lighting shadow puppets. The answer is to have a reflector board hung at a suitable angle above the puppeteers' heads and shine a number of spotlights on it. With this technique there will be no rod shadows, but it will be necessary to keep the figures pressed hard against the screen in order to get a sharp image. There are certain advantages in a cotton screen with this in mind, as the slight stretch allows it to mould itself round the puppets. But generally speaking frosted plastic is better as it disperses the light so well. It is helpful to have the screen tilted slightly forwards, so that figures tend to lie against it.

It may seem that manipulating shadow puppets is a purely mechanical business; not a bit of it. The good player throws himself into his part whatever he is playing, and this sincerity and sense of timing most definitely has its effect on the audience, though they may not realise it. As for the Chinese, who not only have three rods for each figure and frequently work one puppet in each hand, sometimes with a string attached to a ring running down a rod to work perhaps a mouth movement, this is almost a juggling feat which they are able to achieve with their long nimble fingers and years of practice – an art in itself.

Marionettes

Marionettes are one of the most complete forms of puppet and are capable of the widest range of performance both in regard to their presentation and in the material they can handle – from Variety to Shakespeare, dance to a straight drama, realism to surrealism, stylisation to fantasy. They may be anything from 25cm (10in) or less to 90 or 122cm (3 or 4ft) high. Ramon Bufano in the USA once presented *Oedipus Rex* with 3m (10ft) figures. Manipulators may be seen by the audience or hidden behind what is now often regarded as an 'old-fashioned' proscenium. Despite the fact that their potential is so great it is not often that one sees really first-class manipulation. For unlike the rod, shadow and glove puppets, not only is a well-balanced and jointed marionette difficult to make, but a very considerable amount of practice and skill is necessary to control it. It is, like playing an instrument, an art that necessitates constant practice, and one should continue working at it for several years. There are people who, after trying their hand briefly or perhaps after witnessing a disappointing show, believe that positive and meaningful manipulation is not possible with marionettes. Even practice, however, does not make perfect for, as for all puppets, one also has to have the right histrionic talent and an actor's feeling for the work.

All the big troupes of a hundred years or more ago used puppets about 90cm (3ft) high. They generally had papier-mâché heads with glass eyes let in. The neck would be part of the head, either a round piece of wood glued in, or part of the wooden shape on which the head was modelled. This would be jointed in a shallow valley in the wooden shoulder-piece by means of large staples or screw-eyes. The shoulder-piece would often be covered in material and made part of a stuffed body, jointed at the waist by tape to a stuffed pelvis. Sometimes these body-pieces would be made in papier-mâché and be hollow. Solid wooden bodies were generally avoided as being too heavy. The arms were stuffed sausages, with tape for the elbow joints and shoulder joints. But the hands were made of wood, plugged into the lower sausages usually with no wrist joint (though of course there would be a certain amount of play in the stuffing). The upper legs were also stuffed tubes attached to the pelvis by broad tapes, but normally the lower leg and foot were of wood. The knee joint in a marionette is extremely important and simply must be made to work as a human knee does, no more and no less; it is generally made in wood, so that the lower part of the upper leg ends in a shaped wooden tongue. Fig 2 shows two ways of making a satisfactory knee joint. These large puppets had no ankle joint. It is interesting that puppet designers usually make the heads larger than human proportions dictate, and the smaller the puppet often the larger in proportion the head, in order that

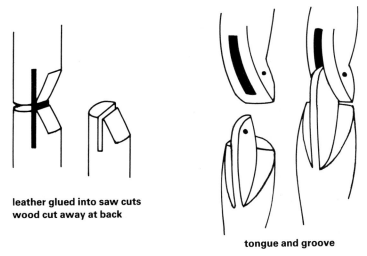

**leather glued into saw cuts
wood cut away at back**

tongue and groove

Fig 2   Knee joints

141

expression and character may carry across the footlights.

Most modern marionettes seem to vary between 45 and 60cm (18 and 24in) high. They are generally made of wood throughout, and often have more joints than the larger ones. The neck may have a double joint, not only at the shoulder, but protruding into the head which is hollowed out, behind the jaw, fixed there by a pin through a screw-eye. A length of round leather belting glued in makes a very good waist joint. Most have wrist joints, a tongue on the end of the hand going into a groove on the arm or a screw-eye going into a hole drilled in the arm, or a short length of leather bootlace glued into both. But care should be taken not to allow too much movement in the wrist. Likewise tongue and groove ankle joints are a help for a walking puppet, so long as the toe doesn't drop too far. A pointed toe is good for a dancer, but only the slightest movement is needed for the ordinary puppet, and the feet should be made to point outwards, otherwise they can trip each other up. Sometimes lead soles are added to counteract stiffness of costume on small figures. There are innumerable different joints possible and the experienced craftsman will choose those which are going to provide the particular movements each puppet will be required to make.

There are also many ways of stringing a marionette, and each perch

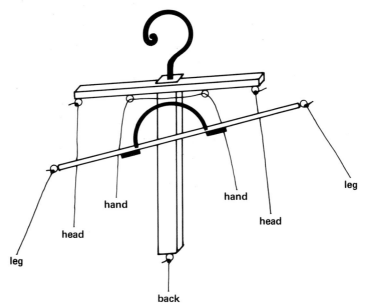

Fig 3   Perch for larger marionettes; loose leg bar hangs by wire loop on wire hook

142

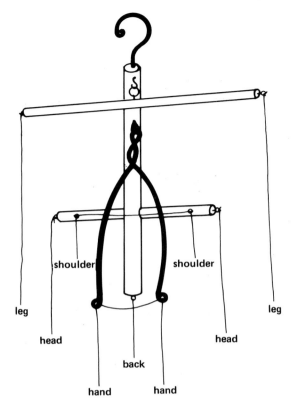

Fig 4 Upright perch for 45 to 60cm (18 to 24in) marionette

should be made to suit its particular character – otherwise they are all going to move in the same way, and the result may be efficient but dull. We show (Figs 3, 4 and 5) four different kinds of perch. The T-shape is suggested for the 90cm (3ft) puppets, the other upright one for the 45 or 50cm (18 or 20in) puppets and the horizontal cross for very small figures. The more elaborate horizontal perch with the two crossbars is for animals (Fig 6). When stringing a puppet all the strings should be taut when the perch is in its normal position and the puppet is standing at rest. Head strings are fixed (usually with screw-eyes) just above the ears. The optimum position must be found so that the puppet is not looking down or up. We do not usually use shoulder strings unless the puppet is very heavy or unless, as in the case of an elderly character, the head is thrust slightly forward. If used, they should be made 'run-through' strings (ie a loop going from one shoulder, through two screw-eyes on the main bar a little way in from the head strings and down to the other shoulder). Sometimes hip strings are added for a speciality

143

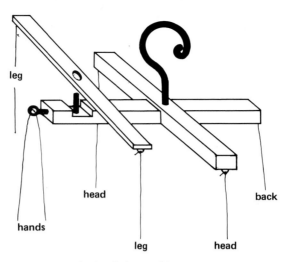

Fig 5   Perch for small marionette

dancer, and these can be tied on the positions shown for the head strings, which can now be made 'run-through' and positioned as described for shoulder strings. The back string is fastened at the small of the back. If a very deep bow is required this can also be made a 'run-through' string, with the other end going to the puppet's bottom.

Hand strings can be placed in a variety of positions according to requirements. A small hole drilled through the hand just inside the thumb gives a natural general movement, but some people prefer a hole through the palm of the hand. The string is threaded through and a double knot tied at the end to stop it pulling out. For hands we also recommend a run-through string, so that you can work either or both hands according to how you pull it. But for certain effects, such as for a pianist or a juggler, it is necessary to have the hand strings on a separate bar. The leg strings are fastened just above the knee joint, either by drilling a hole through the leg or putting in a screw-eye. There are advantages in screw-eyes: if a string happens to break during a performance it is much quicker to replace it through a screw-eye than having to thread it through a small hole; but as is so often the case, what is practical for stage purposes doesn't always look so neat close to.

Leg strings go to a detachable leg bar, a leg on either end, except in the case of animals (Fig 6) when the detachable piece is generally that for the head and mouth. Various other strings can be added with experience and necessity, elbow strings, toe strings, nose strings (to make a puppet look up), strings to bring a hand to the chest, or take a handkerchief out of a pocket etc, etc. A mouth string when used (and as we have

144

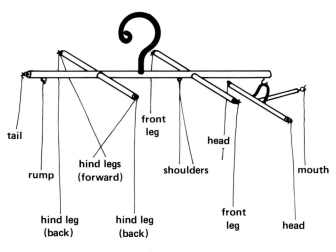

tail

front
leg

head

hind legs
(forward)

rump

shoulders

mouth

hind leg
(back)

hind leg
(back)

front
leg

head

Fig 6   Animal perch

said before we only recommend mouth movement in very special cir-
cumstances), is generally placed in a position where one of the fingers of
the hand holding the main perch – often the little finger – can tweak it.
The mouth is weighted inside the puppet so that it rests in a closed position, and the string working it runs through a hole inside the puppet's
head. We do not, however, generally weight animal mouths but let
them fall open by their own weight. Adjustment of the angle of the wire
loop from which the mouth and head triangle hangs, will create a spring
to keep the mouth closed. The string is fixed on the lower jaw and runs
through a hole in the roof of the mouth.

When practising manipulation a mirror is a great help, but one must
be careful not to rely on this, for it won't be there in the performance.
One must learn to interpret the marionette's attitude partly from a
bird's-eye view and partly by feel. When it comes to actual rehearsal it is
essential to have someone as producer, because one can often make
wrong gestures or movements, for example raising an arm far too high.
The greatest difficulty is to keep the figure at the right height, neither
floating in the air nor sagging at the knees, and this is really a question of
just feeling the weight in one's wrist, just the lightest touch of the puppet's feet on the floor. When handling a marionette wearing a long skirt
or robe this is in fact one's only guide. Practise by just holding the figure
upright and bouncing it gently on the floor until you can feel its ankle
joints come into play. Walking is the most difficult thing to make a
marionette do, so don't attempt it straight away. Practise arm gestures
and body attitudes. By twisting the perch sharply the head can be made

to turn and, if the perch is tilted forward, the puppet will bow. With the back string slightly tensed the head can be made to look from side to side, as if seeking something, by rocking the perch. For a deeper bow the free hand can take the weight on the back string as the perch is lowered.

The T-type perch (Fig 3) is operated with the leg bar taken off and held in the free hand, with which the hand strings or any other special strings on the main bar can be plucked. The perch for the middle-sized figures should be held with the hand wire resting on the middle finger so that the arms can be kept alive, the free hand being used to pull an individual string for a specific gesture. With this type of perch it is possible to place the first finger and thumb over the leg bar while it is still hooked on, to make the figure take an odd step or two. But for walking or dancing with any type of perch, the leg bar must be taken off, held in the middle with the hand over the top, and rocked like a see-saw, giving an equal pull to each leg. Before walking try dancing. To learn the standard marionette dance movement bounce the figure rhythmically on both feet. When your wrist is accustomed to the movement start raising one leg at a time whilst keeping the bounce going, as follows: both feet down, hop on left foot, both feet down, hop on right foot, both feet down, hop on left foot etc.

To get a good walk, the leg bar should be held well in front of the main perch. A very slight bounce on the figure as each step is taken helps, and often a fairly quick walk is more successful than a beginner's slow motion effort. Don't forget that the puppet must walk in both directions. Whichever hand you find easiest for holding the main control it is better when turning to walk back not to change hands, which may cause the puppet to have convulsions, but to get accustomed to crossing your arms so that the leg bar remains well in front of the control. With animals, with fixed leg bars, you can change hands.

These movements must be practised and practised over and over again until they become second nature, and quite automatic. In making a marionette move one must no more think of which string should be pulled than decide which particular muscles in your own body you should call into play when moving yourself.

There are many other types of control besides those described here. Each puppeteer has his own favourite variation. The experienced manipulator will be able to handle the most unusual after a very short time. An Italian showman once said to us when we were comparing notes about this: 'Bah! I am a puppet master. Give me a bunch of strings in my hands and I will make the puppet live.'

Fig 7   Set-up for small marionette stage with proscenium masking cut away

We have already described some of the different ways a marionette show can be staged. For the general principle see Fig 7. It is worth noting that with long strings from a high bridge one does get a slightly less jerky movement, owing to the stretch of the string; but the puppets are more difficult to control, tending to twist, and it is usually necessary for a floor assistant to steady them for their entrances. The shorter the strings, naturally the greater the leverage power of the perch. Never use transparent nylon for the strings. Not only does it become conspicuous by catching the light, but it is very stretchy and will not stay 'tuned'. It is also slippery to handle and very hard to tie in a secure knot. Linen thread of various thicknesses is best.

Whilst one does not want to thrust the strings in an audience's eyes, invisibility is also unsatisfactory. A marionette does not seem complete without its strings to explain its movement. The old showmen generally used a dark green as being a good average colour to blend in with the

147

scenery. For some special film effects it is important that the strings should not be seen. For example we were commissioned to provide a lion for the film *Simba* which had to attack a man cowering under a tree in the bush. We made a very realistic looking puppet and strung it on very fine wire. When these shots were cut in with close-ups of a real lion the effect was most successful. For close-up work on TV, ordinary theatrical stringing will look too rope-like and performers often make special duplicate figures, or perhaps just a head and shoulders, for close-ups, rather than restring a figure with fine strings that could break at a crucial moment.

But all this practical advice is of no avail unless someone who can act is going to work the puppet. The whole essence of manipulating any kind of puppet is acting. A puppet can be described as an actor's make-up through which he portrays a character study, and through which he expresses himself. It is a tool, a dead thing until handled by an artist. Let us close with words by Gordon Craig from his chapbook *Puppets and Poets*. 'The wood is much, the wires, the stage, the whole technique very much – but far more important is who it is that is holding the puppet.'

FURTHER INFORMATION

The Puppet Centre
The Administrator, Battersea Arts Centre, Lavender Hill,
London SW11 5TJ

The Puppet Centre has a library for use on the premises and will supply list of books for sale. It issues a publication *Animations* six times a year and organises courses etc in all types of puppet activity.

The British Puppet & Model Theatre Guild
The Secretary, 18 Maple Road, Yeading, Hayes, Middlesex

The Guild has a library and will send books out to members. It holds regular meetings in London and occasionally in other places, and runs weekend seminars. It issues a monthly newsletter and a publication *The Puppet Master* once or twice a year.

British UNIMA (Union Internationale de la Marionette)
Secretary, 5 Greystoke Gardens, Oakwood, Enfield

British UNIMA issues a quarterly Bulletin (including reviews of new puppet publications) and supplies information regarding international festivals and other activities.

We have to sound a word of warning: it is illegal to use recorded music without a licence. In fact one needs two licences; one with Phono-graphic Performance Ltd for the use of disc or tape, and one with the Performing Rights Society for the use of the actual music. It is also illegal to re-record music without a licence, eg from disc to tape, though permission can be given for home convenience. Most commercial theatres will carry the necessary licences, but it is up to you to check, and report to them what music you are using.

The quotation 'O Lord let me be a Wayang in your hands' by the Javanese poet Noto Suroto on page 28 is from *Art of the World – Indonesia*, by kind permission of Methuen & Co.

INDEX